# LYRICS AND OTHER POEMS.

Merry Christmas to
Floy, from
Aunt Nannie.

1885.

# LYRICS AND OTHER POEMS,

BY

RICHARD WATSON GILDER.

*I. LYRICS AND HYMNS.*

*II. BALLADS.*

*III. SONNETS.*

*IV. ODES AND MEDITATIVE POEMS.*

*V. THE NEW DAY.*

NEW YORK:
CHARLES SCRIBNER'S SONS.
1885.

# CONTENTS.

LYRICS. PAGE.

BALLADS.



SONNETS.

## ODES AND MEDITATIVE POEMS.

# THE NEW DAY.

## PART III.

## PART IV.

# LYRICS.

## A CHRISTMAS HYMN.

I.

TELL me what is this innumerable throng
Singing in the heavens a loud angelic song?
These are they who come with swift and shining feet
From round about the throne of God the Lord of Light to greet.

II.

Oh, who are these that hasten beneath the starry sky —
As if with joyful tidings that through the world shall fly? —

The fearful shepherds these, who greatly were afeared
When, as they watched their flocks by night, the heavenly host appeared.

III.

Who are these that follow across the hills of night
A star that westward hurries along the fields of light?
Three wise men from the East who myrrh and treasure bring
To lay them at the feet of him their Lord and Christ and King.

IV.

What babe new-born is this that in a manger cries?
Near on her lowly bed his happy mother lies.
Oh, see the air is shaken with white and heavenly wings —
This is the Lord of all the earth, this is the King of Kings.

## HYMN:

SUNG AT THE PRESENTATION OF THE OBELISK TO THE CITY OF NEW YORK, FEB. 22, 1881.

I.

GREAT GOD, to whom since time began
The world has prayed and striven;
Maker of stars, and earth, and man —
To thee our praise is given.
Here, by this ancient Sign
Of thine own Light divine,
We lift to thee our eyes
Thou Dweller of the Skies,—
Hear us, O God in Heaven!

II.

Older than Nilus' mighty flood
Into the Mid-Sea pouring,

Or than the sea, thou God hast stood,—
  Thou God of our adoring!
    Waters and stormy blast
    Haste when thou bid'st them haste;
    Silent, and hid, and still,
    Thou sendest good and ill:
  Thy ways are past exploring.

III.

In myriad forms, by myriad names,
  Men seek to bind and mould thee;
But thou dost melt, like wax in flames,
  The cords that would enfold thee.
    Who madest life and light,
    Bring'st morning after night,
    Who all things did'st create—
    No majesty, nor state,
  Nor word, nor world, can hold thee!

IV.

Great God, to whom since time began
  The world has prayed and striven;

Maker of stars, and earth, and man—
To thee our praise is given.
Of suns thou art the Sun,—
Eternal, holy One:
Who can us help save thou!
To thee alone we bow!
Hear us, O God in Heaven!

## MORNING AND NIGHT.

THE mountain that the morn doth kiss
  Glad greets its shining neighbor:
Lord! heed the homage of our bliss,—
  The incense of our labor.

Now the long shadows eastward creep,
  The golden sun is setting:
Take, Lord! the worship of our sleep,—
  The praise of our forgetting.

## A SONG OF EARLY SUMMER.

Not yet the orchard lifted
  Its cloudy bloom to the sky,
Nor through the twilight drifted
  The whip-poor-will's low cry;

The gray rock had not made
  Of the vine its glistening kirtle;
Nor shook in the locust shade
  The purple bells of the myrtle.

Not yet up the chimney-hollow
  Was heard in the darkling night
The boom and whir of the swallow
  And the twitter that follows the flight;

Before the foamy whitening
  Of the water below the mill;
Ere yet the summer lightning
  Shone red at the edge of the hill —

In the time of sun and showers,
  Of skies half-black, half-clear;
'Twixt melting snows and flowers;
  At the poise of the flying year;

When woods flushed pink and yellow
  In dreams of leafy June;
And days were keen or mellow
  Like tones in a changing tune—

Before the birds had broken
  Forth in their song divine,
Oh! then the word was spoken
  That made my darling mine.

## A MIDSUMMER SONG.

Oh, father 's gone to market-town, he was up before
the day,
And Jamie 's after robins, and the man is making
hay,
And whistling down the hollow goes the boy that
minds the mill,
While mother from the kitchen-door is calling with
a will,
"Polly!—Polly!—The cows are in the corn!
Oh, where 's Polly?"

From all the misty morning air there comes a summer
sound,—
A murmur as of waters from skies, and trees and
ground.
The birds they sing upon the wing, the pigeons bill
and coo,
And over hill and hollow rings again the loud halloo:
"Polly!—Polly!—The cows are in the corn!
Oh, where 's Polly?"

Above the trees the honey-bees swarm by with buzz
and boom,
And in the field and garden a thousand blossoms
bloom.
Within the farmer's meadow a brown-eyed daisy blows,
And down at the edge of the hollow a red and
thorny rose.
But Polly! — Polly! — The cows are in the corn!
Oh, where 's Polly?

How strange at such a time of day the mill should
stop its clatter!
The farmer's wife is listening now and wonders what 's
the matter.
Oh, wild the birds are singing in the wood and on
the hill,
While whistling up the hollow goes the boy that
minds the mill.
But Polly! — Polly! — The cows are in the corn!
Oh, where 's Polly?

## "ON THE WILD ROSE TREE."

On the wild rose tree
Many buds there be,
Yet each sunny hour
Hath but one perfect flower.

Thou who wouldst be wise
Open wide thine eyes,—
In each sunny hour
Pluck the one perfect flower!

## A SONG OF EARLY AUTUMN.

WHEN late in summer the streams run yellow,
  Burst the bridges and spread into bays;
When berries are black and peaches are mellow,
  And hills are hidden by rainy haze;

When the golden-rod is golden still,
  But the heart of the sun-flower is darker and sadder;
When the corn is in stacks on the slope of the hill,
  And slides o'er the path the stripéd adder.

When butterflies flutter from clover to thicket,
  Or wave their wings on the drooping leaf;
When the breeze comes shrill with the call of the cricket—
  Grasshoppers' rasp, and rustle of sheaf.

When high in the field the fern-leaves wrinkle,
  And brown is the grass where the mowers have mown;
When low in the meadow the cow-bells tinkle,
  And small brooks crinkle o'er stock and stone.

When heavy and hollow the robin's whistle,
  And shadows are deep in the heat of noon;
When the air is white with the down o' the thistle,
  And the sky is red with the harvest moon;

Oh then be chary, young Robert and Mary,
  No time let slip, not a moment wait!
    If the fiddle would play it must stop its tuning,
    And they who would wed must be done with
        their mooning.
Let the churn rattle, see well to the cattle,
  And pile the wood by the barn-yard gate!

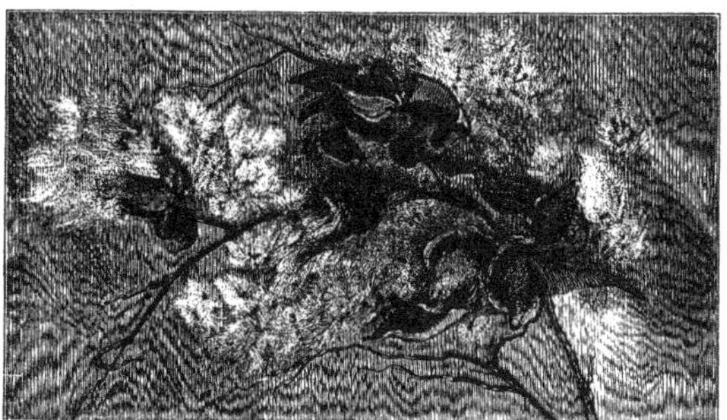

## A WOMAN'S THOUGHT.

I AM a woman—therefore I may not
Call to him, cry to him,
Fly to him,
Bid him delay not!

And when he comes to me, I must sit quiet:
Still as a stone—
All silent and cold.
If my heart riot—
Crush and defy it!
Should I grow bold—
Say one dear thing to him,
All my life fling to him,
Cling to him—
What to atone
Is enough for my sinning!

This were the cost to me,
This were my winning—
That he were lost to me.

Not as a lover
At last if he part from me,
Tearing my heart from me—
Hurt beyond cure,—
Calm and demure
Then must I hold me—
In myself fold me—
Lest he discover;
Showing no sign to him
By look of mine to him
What he has been to me—
How my heart turns to him,
Follows him, yearns to him,
Prays him to love me.

Pity me, lean to me,
Thou God above me!

## " A WORD SAID IN THE DARK."

A WORD said in the dark
And hands pressed, for a token;
" Now, little maiden, mark
The word that you have spoken;
Be not your promise broken ! "

His lips upon her cheek
Felt tears among their kisses;
" O pardon I bespeak
If for my doubting this is !
Now all my doubting ceases."

## "AFTER SORROW'S NIGHT."

AFTER sorrow's night
Dawned the morning bright.
In dewy woods I heard
A golden-throated bird,
    And " Love, love, love," it sang,
        And " Love, love, love."

Evening shadows fell
In our happy dell.
From glimmering woods I heard
A golden-throated bird,
    And " Love, love, love," it sang,
        And " Love, love, love."

Oh, the summer night
Starry was and bright.
In the dark woods I heard
A golden-throated bird,
    And " Love, love, love," it sang,
        And " Love, love, love."

## BEFORE SUNRISE.

THE winds of morning move and sing,
The western stars are lingering;
In the pale east one planet still
Shines large above King Philip's hill;—

And near, in gold against the blue,
The old moon, in its arms the new.
Lo, the deep waters of the bay
Stir with the breath of hurrying day.

Wake, loved one, wake and look with me
Across the narrow, dawn-lit sea!
Such beauty is not wholly mine
Till thou, dear heart, hast made it thine.

## "THE WOODS THAT BRING THE SUNSET NEAR."

THE wind from out the west is blowing,
The homeward-wandering cows are lowing,
Dark grow the pine-woods, dark and drear,—
The woods that bring the sunset near.

When o'er wide seas the sun declines,
Far off its fading glory shines,
Far off, sublime, and full of fear —
The pine-woods bring the sunset near.

This house that looks to east, to west,
This, dear one, is our home, our rest;
Yonder the stormy sea, and here
The woods that bring the sunset near.

## "O SILVER RIVER FLOWING TO THE SEA."

O SILVER river flowing to the sea,
Strong, calm, and solemn as thy mountains be!
Poets have sung thy ever-living power,
Thy wintry day, and summer sunset hour;
Have told how rich thou art, how broad, how deep;
What commerce thine, how many myriads reap
The harvest of thy waters. They have sung
Thy moony nights, when every shadow flung
From cliff or pine is peopled with dim ghosts
Of settlers, old-world fairies, or the hosts
Of Indian warriors that once ploughed thy waves—
Now hurrying to the dance from hidden graves;
The waving outline of thy wooded mountains,
Thy populous towns that stretch from forest fountains
On either side, far to the salty main,
Like golden coins alternate on a chain.

Thou pathway of the empire of the North,
Thy praises through the earth have travelled forth!
I hear thee praised as one who hears the shout
That follows when a hero from the rout
Of battle issues, "Lo, how brave is he,—
How noble, proud, and beautiful!" But she
Who knows him best—"How tender!" So thou art
The river of love to me!
— Heart of my heart,
Dear love and bride—is it not so indeed?—
Among your treasures keep this new-plucked reed.

---

## "BACK FROM THE DARKNESS TO THE LIGHT AGAIN."

"Back from the darkness to the light again!"—
Not from the darkness, Love, for hadst thou lain
Within the shadowy portal of the tomb,
Thy light had warmed the darkness into bloom.

## "O LOVE IN SORROW!"

O Love in sorrow! sorrow, Love, no more;
Though dark the night, the morning cometh fast:
Though black the ocean, bright the circling shore.

Not long we labor at the wearying oar,
For lo! strong love upholds the fallen mast:
The storm but hurries us where we would be—
Beyond the driving winds and raging sea.

## "THE SMILE OF HER I LOVE."

The smile of her I love is like the dawn
Whose touch makes Memnon sing:
O see where wide the golden sunlight flows—
The barren desert blossoms as the rose!

The smile of her I love—when that is gone,
O'er all the world night spreads her shadowy wing.

## AT NIGHT.

THE sky is dark, and dark the bay below
Save where the midnight city's pallid glow
    Lies like a lily white
    On the black pool of night.

O rushing steamer, hurry on thy way
Across the swirling Kills and gusty bay,
    To where the eddying tide
    Strikes hard the city's side!

For there, between the river and the sea,
Beneath that glow,—the lily's heart to me,—
    A sleeping mother mild,
    And by her breast a child.

## CRADLE SONG.

In the embers shining bright
A garden grows for thy delight,
With roses yellow, red, and white.

But, O my child, beware, beware!
Touch not the roses growing there,
For every rose a thorn doth bear.

## NINE YEARS.

Nine years to heaven had flown,
  And June came, with June's token —
The wild rose that had known
  A maiden's silence broken.

'Twas thus the lover spoke,
  And thus she leaned and listened:
(Below, the billows broke,
  The blue sea shook and glistened,)

"We have been happy, Love,
  Through bright and stormy weather,
Happy all hope above,
  For we have been together.

"To meet, to love, to wed —
  Joy without stint or measure —
This was our lot," he said,
  "To find untouched our treasure.

"But had some blindfold fate
  Bound each unto another—
To turn from Heaven's gate,
  Each heart-throb hide and smother!

"O dear and faithful heart
  If thus had we been fated;
To meet, to know, to part—
  Too early, falsely, mated!

"Were this out bitter plight,
  Ah, could we have dissembled?"
Her cheek turned pale with fright;
  She hid her face, and trembled.

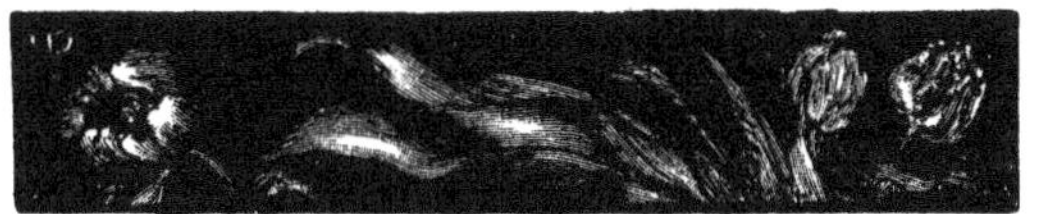

## A NOVEMBER CHILD.

November winds, blow mild
On this new-born child!
Spirit of the autumn wood,
Make her gentle, make her good!
Still attend her,
And befriend her,
Fill her days with warmth and color;
Keep her safe from winter's dolor.
On thy bosom
Hide this blossom
Safe from summer's rain and thunder!
When those eyes of light and wonder
Tire at last of earthly places—
Full of years and full of graces—
Then, O then
Take her back to heaven again!

## REFORM.

I.

OH, how shall I help to right the world that is going wrong!
And what can I do to hurry the promised time of peace!
The day of work is short and the night of sleep is long;
And whether to pray or preach, or whether to sing a song,
To plow in my neighbor's field, or to seek the golden fleece,
Or to sit with my hands in my lap, and wish that ill would cease!

II.

I think, sometimes, it were best just to let the Lord alone;
I am sure some people forget He was here before they came;

Though they say it is all for His glory, 't is a good
deal more for their own,
That they peddle their petty schemes, and blate and
babble and groan.
I sometimes think it were best, and I were little to
blame,
Should I sit with my hands in my lap, in my face
a crimson shame.

## THE VOYAGER.

I.

" FRIEND, why goest thou forth
When ice-hills drift from the north
And crush together ? "

" The Voice that me doth call
Heeds not the ice-hill's fall,
Nor wind, nor weather."

II.

" But, friend, the night is black ;
Behold the driving wrack
And wild seas under ! "

" My straight and narrow bark
Fears not the threatening dark,
Nor storm, nor thunder."

III.

"But oh, thy children dear!
Thy wife—she is not here—
I haste to bring her!"

"No, no, it is too late!
Hush, hush! I may not wait,
Nor weep, nor linger."

IV.

"Hark! Who is he that knocks
With slow and dreadful shocks
The walls to sever?"

"It is my Master's call,
I go, whate'er befall;
Farewell forever."

## DRINKING SONG.

I.

Thou who lov'st and art forsaken,
Didst believe, and wert mistaken,
From thy dream thou wilt not waken
*When Death thee shall call.*
Like are infidel, believer,—
The deceived, and the deceiver,
*When the grave hides all.*

II.

What if thou be saint or sinner,
Crooked gray-beard, straight beginner,—
Empty paunch, or jolly dinner,
*When Death thee shall call.*
All alike are rich and richer,
King with crown, and cross-legged stitcher.
*When the grave hides all.*

III.

Hope not thou to live hereafter
In men's memories and laughter,
When, 'twixt hearth and ringing rafter,
*Death thee shall call.*
For we both shall be forgotten,
Friend, when thou and I are rotten
*And the grave hides all.*

## DECORATION DAY.

I.

SHE saw the bayonets flashing in the sun,
The flags that proudly waved; she heard the bugles
calling;
She saw the tattered banners falling
About the broken staffs, as one by one
The remnant of the mighty army passed;
And at the last
Flowers for the graves of those whose fight was done.

II.

She heard the tramping of ten thousand feet
As the long line swept round the crowded square;
She heard the incessant hum
That filled the warm and blossom-scented air,—
The shrilling fife, the roll and throb of drum,

The happy laugh, the cheer.—Oh glorious and meet
To honor thus the dead,
Who chose the better part
And for their country bled!
—The dead! Great God! she stood there in the street,
Living, yet dead in soul and mind and heart—
While far away
His grave was decked with flowers by strangers' hands to-day.

New York, May 30, 1877.

---

## NORTH TO THE SOUTH.

Land of the South, whose stricken heart and brow
Bring grief to eyes that erewhile only knew
For their own loss to sorrow,—spurn not thou
These tribute tears,—ah, we have suffered too.

New Orleans, 1885.

## THE DEAD COMRADE.

At the burial of Grant, a bugler stood forth and sounded "taps."

I.

Come, soldiers, arouse ye!
Another has gone;
Let us bury our comrade,
His battles are done.
    His sun it is set;
He was true, he was brave,
He feared not the grave,
There is nought to regret.

II.

Bring music and banners
And wreaths for his bier,—
No fault of the fighter
That Death conquered here.
    Bring him home ne'er to rove,
Bear him home to his rest,
And over his breast
Fold the flag of his love.

III.

Great Captain of battles,
We leave him with thee!
What was wrong, O forgive it;
His spirit make free.
    Sound taps, and away!
Out lights, and to bed!
Farewell, soldier dead!
Farewell — for a day.

## PORTO FINO.

I KNOW a girl — she is a poet's daughter,
  And many-mooded as a poet's day,
And changing as the Mediterranean water;
  We walked together by an emerald bay,

So deep, so green, so promontory-hidden
  That the lost mariner might peer in vain
Through storms, to find where he erewhile had ridden,
  Safe-sheltered from the wild and windy main.

Down the high stairs we clambered just to rest a
  Cool moment in the church's antique shade.
How gay the aisles and altars! 'Twas the festa
  Of brave Saint George who the old dragon laid.

How bright the little port! The red flags fluttered,
  Loud clanged the bells, and loud the children's glee:
What though some distant, unseen storm-cloud muttered,
  And waves breathed big along the weedy quay.

We climbed the hill whose rising cleaves asunder
  Green bay and blue immeasurable sea;
We heard the breakers at its bases thunder;
  We heard the priests' harsh chant soar wild and free.

Then through the graveyard's straight and narrow portal
  Our journey led. How dark the place! How strange
Its steep, black mountain walls,—as if the immortal
  Spirit could thus be stayed its skyward range!

Beyond, the smoky olives clothed the mountains
  In green that grew through many a moon-lit night.
Below, down cleft and chasm leaped snowy fountains;
  Above, the sky was warm, and blue, and bright;

When, sudden, from out a fair and smiling heaven
  Burst forth the rain, quick as a trumpet-blare:
Yet still the Italian sun each drop did leaven,
  And turned the rain to diamonds in the air.

So passed the day in shade, and shower, and sun,
  Like thine own moods, thou sweet and changeful maiden!
Great Heaven! deal kindly with this gentle one,
  Nor let her soul too heavily be laden.

## A MADONNA OF FRA LIPPO LIPPI.

No heavenly maid we here behold,
Though round her brow a ring of gold;
This baby, solemn-eyed and sweet,
Is human all from head to feet.

Together close her palms are prest
In worship of that godly guest:
But glad her heart and unafraid
While on her neck his hand is laid.

Two children, happy, laughing, gay,
Uphold the little child in play:
Not flying angels these, what though
Four wings from their four shoulders grow.

Fra Lippo, we have learned from thee
A lesson of humanity:
To every mother's heart forlorn,
In every house the Christ is born.

## ESSIPOFF.

I.

WHAT is her playing like?
I ask—while dreaming here under her music's power.
'T is like the leaves of the dark passion-flower
Which grows on a strong vine whose roots, oh deep
they sink,
Deep in the ground, that flower 's pure life to drink.

II.

What is her playing like?
'T is like a bird
Who, singing in a wild wood, never knows
That its lone melody is heard
By wandering mortal, who forgets his heavy woes.

## "WE MET UPON THE CROWDED WAY."

I.

We met upon the crowded way;
We spoke and passed. How bright the day
Turned from that moment, for a light
Did shine from her to make it bright!
And then I asked: Can such as she
From life be blotted utterly?
The thoughts from those clear eyes that dawn—
Down to the ground can they be drawn?

II.

Among the mighty who can find
One that hath a perfect mind?
Angry, jealous, cursed by feuds,—
They own the sway of fatal moods;
But thou dost perfect seem to me
In thy divine simplicity.
Though from the heavens the stars be wrenched,
Thy light, dear maid, shall not be quenched.
Gentle, and true, and pure, and free—
The gods will not abandon thee!

## FOR AN ALBUM.

(TO BE READ ONE HUNDRED YEARS AFTER.)

A CENTURY'S summer breezes shook
The maple shadows on the grass
Since she who owned this ancient book
From the green world to heaven did pass.

Beside a northern lake she grew,
A wild-flower on its craggy walls;
Her eyes were mingled gray and blue,
Like waves where summer sunlight falls.

Cheerful from morn to evening-close,
No humblest work, no prayer forgot:
Yet who of woman born but knows
The sorrows of our mortal lot!

And she too suffered, though the wound
Was hidden from the general gaze,

And most from those who thus had found
An added burden for their days.

She had no special grace, nor art;
Her riches not in banks were kept:
Her treasure was a gentle heart,
Her skill to comfort those who wept.

Not without foes her days were passed,
For quick her burning scorn was fanned.
Her friends were many — least and last,
A poet from a distant land.

---

## STREPHON AND SARDON.

"YOUNG Strephon wears his heart upon his sleeve,"
Thus wizened Sardon spoke, with scoffing air;
Perhaps 'twas envy made the gray-beard grieve —
For Sardon never had a heart to wear.

## THE POET'S PROTEST.

O MAN with your rule and measure,
  Your tests and analyses!
You may take your empty pleasure,
  May kill the pine, if you please;
You may count the rings and the seasons,
  May hold the sap to the sun,
You may guess at the ways and the reasons
  Till your little day is done.

But for me the golden crest
  That shakes in the wind and launches
Its spear toward the reddening West!
  For me the bough and the breeze,
The sap unseen, and the glint
  Of light on the dew-wet branches,—
The hiding shadows, the hint
  Of the soul of mysteries.

You may sound the sources of life,
  And prate of its aim and scope;
You may search with your chilly knife
  Through the broken heart of hope.
But for me the love-sweet breath,
  And the warm, white bosom heaving,
And never a thought of death,
  And only the bliss of living.

---

## WANTED, A THEME!

"Give me a theme," the little poet cried,
  "And I will do my part."
"'T is not a theme you need," the world replied;
  "You need a heart."

## "WHEN THE TRUE POET COMES."

"When the true poet comes, how shall we know him?
By what clear token,—manners, language, dress?
Or will a voice from heaven speak and show him,—
Him the swift healer of the earth's distress?
Tell us, that when the long-expected comes
At last, with mirth and melody and singing,
We him may greet with banners, beat of drums,
Welcome of men and maids and joybells ringing:
And, for this poet of ours,
Laurels and flowers."

Thus shall ye know him, this shall be his token,—
Manners like other men, an unstrange gear,
His speech not musical, but harsh and broken
Will sound at first, each line a driven spear.

For he will sing as in the centuries olden,
  Before mankind its earliest fire forgot—
Yet whoso listens long hears music golden.
  —How shall ye know him? Ye shall know him not
      Till, ended hate and scorn,
      To the grave he's borne.

---

## TO A YOUNG POET.

IN the morning of the skies
I heard a lark arise.
On the first day of the year
A wood-flower did appear.

Like a violet, like a lark,
Like the dawn that kills the dark,
Like a dew-drop, trembling, clinging,
Is the poet's first sweet singing.

## DESECRATION.

THE poet died last night;
  Outworn his mortal frame.
He hath fought well the fight,
  And won a deathless name.

Bring laurel for his bier,
  And flowers to deck the hearse.
The tribute of a tear
  To his immortal verse.

Hushed is that piercing strain,—
  Who heard, for pleasure wept.
His were our joy and pain:
  He sang — our sorrow slept.

Yes, weep for him; no more
  Shall such high songs have birth:
Gone is the harp he bore
  Forever from the earth.

Weep, weep, and scatter flowers
  Above his precious dust:
Child of the heavenly powers,—
  Divine, and pure, and just.

Weep, weep — for when to-night
  Doth hoot the horned owl,
Beneath the pale moon's light
  The human ghouls will prowl.

What creatures those will throng
  Within the sacred gloom,
To do our poet wrong —
  To break the sealed tomb?

Not the great world and gay
  That pities not, nor halts
By thoughtless night or day —
  But, O more sordid-false,

His trusted friend and near,
  To whom his spirit moved;
The brother he held dear;
  The woman that he loved.

## YOUTH AND AGE.

I.

"I LIKE your book, my boy,
'Tis full of youth and joy,
And love that sings and dreams.
Yet it puzzles me," he said;
"A string of pearls it seems,—
But I cannot find the thread."

II.

"O friend of olden days!
Dear to me is your praise:
But, many and many a year
You must go back, I fear;
You must journey back," I said,
"To find that golden thread!"

## OUR ELDER POETS.

(1878.)

HE is gone. We shall not see again
  That reverend form, those silver locks;
Silent at last the iron pen
  And words that poured like molten rocks.

He is gone, and we who thought him cold
  Miss from our lives a generous heat,
And know that stolid form did hold
  A fire that burned, a heart that beat.

He is gone, but other bards remain:
  Our gray-old prophet, young at heart,
Our scholar-poet's patriot strain;
  And he of the wise and mellow art.

And he who first to science sought,
  But to the merry muses after;
Who learned a secret never taught—
  The knowledge of men's tears and laughter.

He also in whose music rude
  Our peopled woods and prairies speak,
Resounding, in his modern mood,
  The tragic fury of the Greek.

And he, too, lingers round about
  The darling city of his birth —
The bard whose gray eyes looking out
  Find scarce one peer in all the earth.

## TO AN ENGLISH FRIEND,

### WITH EMERSON'S "POEMS."

EDMUND, in this book you'll find
Music from a prophet's mind.
Even when harsh the numbers be,
There's an inward melody;
And when sound is one with sense,
'Tis a bird's song — sweet, intense.
Chide me not the book is small,
For in it lies our all in all:
We who in Eldorado live
Have no better gift to give.
When no more is silver mill,
Golden stream, or golden hill —
Search the New World from pole to pole,
Here you'll find its very soul!

## "JOCOSERIA."

MEN grow old before their time,
  With the journey half before them:
In languid rhyme
  They deplore them.

Life up-gathers carks and cares,
  So good-bye to maid and lover!
Find three gray hairs,
  And cry, "All's over!"

Look at Browning! How he keeps
  In the seventies still a heart
That never sleeps,—
  Still an art

Full of youth's own grit and power,
  Thoughts we deemed to boys belonging,—
The spring-time's flower,
  Love-and-longing.

## THE MODERN RHYMER.

I.

Now YOU who rhyme, and I who rhyme,
Have not we sworn it, many a time,
That we no more our verse would scrawl,
For Shakespeare he had said it all!
And yet whatever others see
The earth is fresh to you and me —
And birds that sing, and winds that blow,
And blooms that make the country glow,
And lusty swains, and maidens bright,
And clouds by day, and stars by night,
And all the pictures in the skies
That passed before Will Shakespeare's eyes;
Love, hate, and scorn,— frost, fire, and flower,—
On us as well as him have power.
Go to! our spirits shall not be laid,
Silenced and smothered by a shade.
Avon is not the only stream

Can make a poet sing and dream;
Nor are those castles, queens, and kings
The height of sublunary things.

II.

Beneath the false moon's pallid glare,
By the cool fountain in the square
(This gray-green dusty square they set
Where two gigantic highways met)
We hear a music rare and new,
Sweet Shakespeare, was not known to you!
You saw the New World's sun arise:
High up it shines in our own skies.
You saw the ocean from the shore:
Through mid-seas now our ship doth roar,—
A wild, new, teeming world of men
That wakens in the poet's brain
Thoughts that were never thought before
Of hope, and longing, and despair,
Wherein man's never resting race
Westward, still westward, on doth fare,
Doth still subdue, and still aspire,

Or turning on itself doth face
Its own indomitable fire,—
O million-centuried thoughts that make
The Past seem but a shallop's wake!

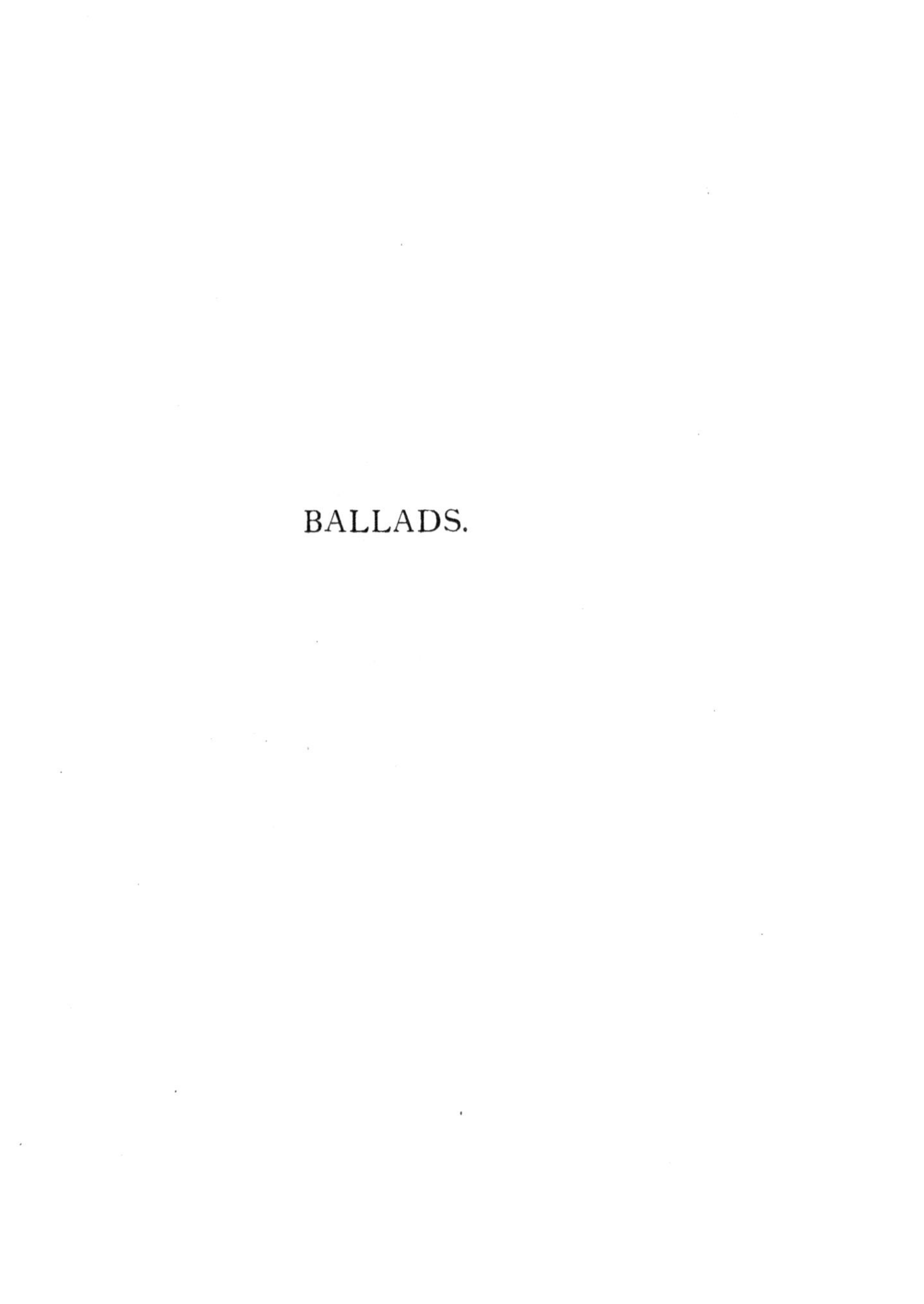

# BALLADS.

# THE RIVER INN.

THE night was black and drear
  Of the last day of the year.
Two guests to the river inn
Came, from the wide world's bound:
One with clangor and din,
The other without a sound.

"Now hurry, servants and host!
Get the best that your cellars boast:
White be the sheets and fine,
And the fire on the hearth-stone bright;
Pile the wood, and spare not the wine,
And call him at morning-light."

"But where is the silent guest?
In what chamber shall she rest?
In this! Should she not go higher?
'Tis damp, and the fire is gone."
"You need not kindle the fire,
You need not call her at dawn."

Next morn he sallied forth
On his journey to the North.
Oh, bright the sunlight shone
Through boughs that the breezes stir;
But for her was lifted a stone
Under the church-yard fir.

## THE WHITE AND THE RED ROSE.

I.

In Heaven's happy bowers
There blossom two flowers,
One with fiery glow
And one as white as snow;
While lo! before them stands,
With pale and trembling hands,
A spirit who must choose
One, and one refuse.

II.

Oh, tell me of these flowers
That bloom in heavenly bowers,
One with fiery glow,
And one as white as snow!
And tell me who is this
In Heaven's holy bliss
Who trembles and who cries
Like a mortal soul that dies!

III.

These blossoms two
Wet with heavenly dew—
The Gentle Heart is one,
And one is Beauty's own;
And the spirit here that stands
With pale and trembling hands—
Before to-morrow's morn
Will be a child new-born,
Will be a mortal maiden
With earthly sorrows laden;
But of these shining flowers
That bloom in heavenly bowers,
To-day she still may choose
One, and one refuse.

IV.

Will she pluck the crimson flower
And win Beauty's dower?
Will she choose the better part

And gain the Gentle Heart?
Awhile she weeping waits
Within those pearly gates;
Alas! the mortal maiden
With earthly sorrow laden;
Her tears afresh they start,—
She has chosen the Gentle Heart.

V.

And now the spirit goes,
In her breast the snow-white rose.
When hark! a voice that calls
Within the garden walls:
"Thou didst choose the better part,
Thou hast won the Gentle Heart,—
Lo, now to thee is given
The red rose of Heaven."

## JOHN CARMAN.

I.

John Carman of Carmantown
  Worked hard through the livelong day;
He drove his awl and he snapped his thread
  And he had but little to say.

He had but little to say
  Except to a neighbor's child:
Three summers old she was, and her eyes
  Had a look that was deep and wild.

Her hair was heavy and brown
  Like clouds in a starry night.
She came and sat by the cobbler's bench
  And his soul was filled with delight.

No kith nor kin had he
  And he never went gadding about;
A strange, shy man, the people said;
  They could not make him out.

And some of them shook their heads
  And would never tell what they'd heard.
But he drove his awl and snapped his thread,—
  And he always kept his word;

And the little child that knew him
  Better than all the rest,
She threw her arms around his neck
  And went to sleep on his breast.

One day in that dreadful summer
  When children died by the score,
John Carman glanced from his work and saw
  Her mother there at the door.

He knew by the look on her face,—
  And his own turned deathly white;
He rose from his bench and followed her out
  And watched by the child that night.

He tended her day and night;
  He watched by her night and day:
He saw the cruel pain in her eyes;
  He saw her lips turn gray.

II.

The day that the child was buried
  John Carman went back to his last,
And the neighbors said that for weeks and weeks
  Not a word his clenched lips passed.

"He takes it hard," they gossiped,
  "Poor man, he's lacking in wit": —
"I'll drop in to-day," said Deacon Gray,
  "And comfort him up a bit."

So Deacon Gray dropped in
  With a kind and neighborly air,
And before he left he knelt on the floor
  And wrestled with God in prayer.

And he said: "O Lord, thou hast stricken
  This soul in its babyhood:
In Thy own way, we beseech and pray,
  Bring forth from evil good."

III.

That night the fire-bells rang
  And the flames shot up to the sky,
And into the street as pale as a sheet
  The town-folk flock and cry.

The bells ring loud and long,
  The flames leap high and higher,
The rattling engines come too late,—
  The old First Church is on fire!

And lo and behold in the lurid glare
  They see John Carman stand,—
A look of mirth on his iron lips
  And a blazing torch in his hand.

"You say it was *He* who killed her"
  (His voice had a fearful sound):
"I'd have you know, who love Him so,
  I've burned his house to the ground."

. . . . .

John Carman died in prison,
  In the madman's cell, they say;
And from his crime, that I've told in rhyme,
  Heaven cleanse his soul, I pray.

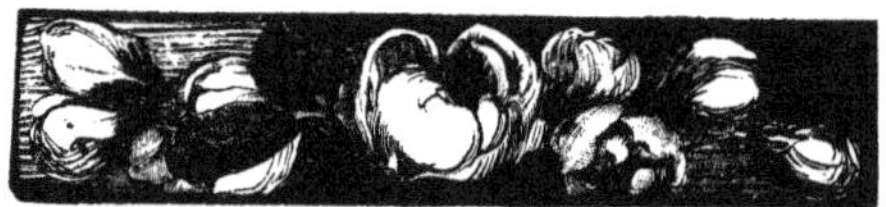

## AT FOUR-SCORE.

This is the house she was born in, full four-score years ago,—
And here she is living still, bowed and ailing, but clinging
Still to this wonted life,—like an ancient and blasted oak-tree,
Whose dying roots yet clasp the ground with an iron hold.

This is the house she was born in, and yonder across the bay
Is the home her lover built,—for her and for him and their children;
Daily she watched it grow, from dawn to the evening twilight,
As it rose on the orchard hill, 'mid the spring-time showers and bloom.

There is the village church, its steeple over the
trees
Rises and shows the clock she has watched since the
day it was started,—
'Tis many a year ago, how many she cannot
remember:
Now solemnly over the water rings out the evening
hour.

And there in that very church,—though, alas, how
bedizened, and changed!
They've painted it up, she says, in their queer, new,
modern fashion,—
There on a morning in June, she gave her hand to her
husband;
Her heart it was his (she told him) long years and
years before.

Now here she sits at the window, gazing out on steeple
and hill;
All but the houses have gone,—the church, and the
trees, and the houses;—

All, all have gone long since, parents, and husband, and children;
And herself—she thinks, at times, she too has vanished and gone.

No, it cannot be she who stood in the church that morning in June,
Nor she who felt at her breast the lips of a child in the darkness:
But hark in the gathering dusk comes a low, quick moan of anguish,—
Ah, it is she indeed, who has lived, who has loved, and lost.

For she thinks of a wintry night, when her last was taken away,
Forty years this very month, the last, the fairest, the dearest;
All gone,—ah, yes, it is she who has loved, who has lost, and suffered,
She and none other it is, left alone in her sorrow and pain.

Still with its sapless roots, that stay though the branches
have dropped,
Have withered, and fallen, and gone, their strength
and their glory forgotten;
Still with the life that remains, silent, and faithful, and
steadfast,
Through sunshine and bending storm clings the oak
to its mother-earth.

## THE BALLAD OF THE CHIMNEY.

I.

My chimney is builded
On a hill by the sea,
At the edge of a wood
That the sunset has gilded
Since time was begun
And the earth first was done:
For mine and for me
And for you, John Burroughs,
My friend old and good,
At the edge of a wood
On a hill by the sea
My chimney is builded.

II.

My chimney gives forth
All its heat to the north,
While its right arm it reaches
Toward the meadows and beaches,
And its left it extends
To its pine-tree friends.
All its heat to the north
My chimney gives forth.

III.

My chimney is builded
Of red and gray granite:
Of great split bowlders
Are its thighs and its shoulders;
Its mouth — try to span it.

'Tis a nine-foot block —
The shelf that hangs over
The stout hearth-rock.

Then the lines they upswell
Like a huge church-bell,
Or a bellying sail
In a stiff south gale
When the ship rolls well,
With a blue sky above her.

IV.

My chimney — come view it,
And I'll tell you, John Burroughs,
What is built into it:
First the derrick's shrill creak,
That perturbed the still air
With a cry of despair;
The lone traveler who passed
At the fall of the night
If he saw not its mast
Stood still with affright
At a sudden strange sound —
Hark! a woman's wild shriek?
Or the baying of a hound?

Then the stone-hammer's clink
And the drill's sharp tinkle,
And bird-songs that sprinkle
Their notes through the wood,
(With pine-odors scented),
On their swift way to drink
At the spring cold and good
That bubbles 'neath the stone
Where the red chieftain tented
In the days that are gone.

Yes, 'twixt granite and mortar
Many songs, long or shorter,
Are imprisoned, I repeat;
And when red leaves shall fall,—
Coming home, all in herds,
From the air to the earth,—
When I have my heart's desire,
And we sit by the hearth
In the glow of the fire,
You and I, John of Birds,
We shall hear as they call

From the gray granite wall,—
You shall name one and all.

There's the crow's caw-cawing
From the pine-tree's height,
And the cat-bird's sawing,
The hissing of the adder
That climbed this rocky ladder,
And the song of Bob White;
The robin's loud clatter,
The chipmunk's chatter,
And the mellow-voiced bell
That the cuckoo strikes well;
Yes, betwixt the stones and in
There is built a merry din.

But not all bright and gay
Are the songs we shall hear;
For as day turns to gray
Comes a voice low and clear—
Whip-poor-will sounds his wail
Over hill, over dale,

Till the soul fills with fright.
'Tis the bird that was heard
On the fields drenched with blood
By the dark southern flood
When they died in the night.

V.

But you cannot split granite,
Howsoever you may plan it,
Without bringing blood —
(There's a drop of mine there
On that block four-square).
Certain oaths, I'm aware,
Sudden, hot, and not good
(May Heaven cleanse the guilt!)
In these stone walls are built —
With the wind through the pine-wood blowing,
The creak of tree on tree,
Child-laughter, and the lowing
Of the homeward-driven cattle,
The sound of wild birds singing,

Of steel on granite ringing,
The memory of battle,
And tales of the roaring sea.

VI.

For my chimney was builded
By a Plymouth County sailor,
An old North Sea whaler.
In the warm noon spell
'Twas good to hear him tell
Of the great September blow
A dozen years ago:
How at dawn of the day
The wind began to play,
Till it cut the waves flat
Like the brim of your hat.
There was no sea about,
But it blew straight out
Till the ship lurched over;
But 'twas quick to recover,
When, all of a stroke,

The hurricane it broke; —
Great heavens! how it roared,
And how the rain poured;
The thirty-fathom chain
Dragged out all in vain.
"What next?" the captain cried
To the mate by his side;
Then Tip Ryder he replied:
"Fetch the axe — no delay —
Cut the main-mast away;
If you want to save the ship
Let the main-mast rip!"
But another said, "Wait!"
And they did — till too late.
On her beam-ends she blew,
In the sea half the crew —
Struggling back through the wrack,
There to cling day and night.
Not a sail heaves in sight;
And, the worst, one in thirst
(Knows no better, the poor lad!)
Drinks salt water and goes mad.

Eighty hours blown and tossed,
Five good sailors drowned and lost,
And the rest brought to shore;
— Some to sail as before;
" Not Tip Ryder, if he starves
Building chimneys, building wharves!"

VII.

Now this was the manner
Of the building of the chimney.
('Tis a good old-timer,
As you, friend John, will own.)
Old man Vail cut the stone;
William Ryder was the builder;
Stanford White was the planner,
And the owner and rhymer
Is Richard Watson Gilder.

# SONNETS.

## THE SONNET.

WHAT is a sonnet? 'Tis the pearly shell
That murmurs of the far-off murmuring sea;
A precious jewel carved most curiously;
It is a little picture painted well.
What is a sonnet? 'Tis the tear that fell
From a great poet's hidden ecstasy;
A two-edged sword, a star, a song — ah me!
Sometimes a heavy-tolling funeral bell.
This was the flame that shook with Dante's breath;
The solemn organ whereon Milton played,
And the clear glass where Shakespeare's shadow falls:
A sea this is — beware who ventureth!
For like a fjord the narrow floor is laid
Mid-ocean deep to the sheer mountain walls.

## LONGFELLOW'S "BOOK OF SONNETS."

'Twas Sunday evening as I wandered down
  The central highway of this swarming place,
  And felt a pleasant stillness,—not a trace
  Of Saturday's harsh turmoil in the town:
Then as a gentle breeze just stirs a gown,
  Yet almost motionless, or as the face
  Of silence smiles, I heard the chimes of "Grace"
  Sound murmuring through the autumn evening's
    brown.
To-day, again, I passed along Broadway
  In the fierce tumult and mid-noise of noon,
  While 'neath my feet the solid pavement shook;
When lo! it seemed that bells began to play
  Upon a Sabbath eve a silver tune,—
  For as I walked I read the poet's book.

## THE NEW TROUBADOURS.

(Avignon, 1879.)

They said that all the troubadours had flown,—
No bird to flash a wing or swell a throat!
But as we journeyed down the rushing Rhone
To Avignon, what joyful note on note
Burst forth beneath thy shadow, O Ventour!
Whose eastward forehead takes the dawn divine:
Ah, dear Provence! ah, happy troubadour,
And that sweet, mellow, antique song of thine!
First Roumanille, the leader of the choir,
Then graceful Matthieu, tender, sighing, glowing,
Then Wyse all fancy, Aubanel all fire,
And Mistral, mighty as the north-wind's blowing;
And youthful Gras, and lo! among the rest
A mother-bird who sang above her nest.

## A SONNET OF DANTE.

*("Tanto gentile e tanto onesta pare.")*

So HIGH and pure my lady as she doth go
  Upon her way, and others doth salute,
  That every tongue becometh trembling-mute,
  And every eye is troubled by that glow.
Her praise she hears as on she moveth slow,
  Clothed with humility as with a suit;
  She seems a thing that came (without dispute)
  From heaven to earth a miracle to show.
Through eyes that gaze on her benignity
  There passes to the heart a sense so sweet
  That none can understand who may not prove;
And from her countenance there seems to move
  A gentle spirit, with all love replete,
  That to the soul comes, saying, "Sigh, O sigh!"

## A RIDDLE OF LOVERS.

Of my fair lady's lovers there were two
  Who loved her more than all; nor she, nor they
  Guessed which of these loved better, for one way
  This had of loving, that another knew.
One round her neck brave arms of empire threw
  And covered her with kisses where she lay:
  The other sat apart, nor did betray
  Sweet sorrow at that sight; but rather drew
His pleasure of his lady through the soul
  And sense of this one. So there truly ran
  Two separate loves through one embrace; the whole
This lady had of both, when one began
  To clasp her close, and win her dear lips' goal.
  Now read my lovers' riddle if you can.

## "WHEN LOVE DAWNED."

WHEN love dawned on that world which is my mind,
  Then did the outer world wherein I went
  Suffer a sudden strange transfigurement,—
  It was as if new sight were given the blind.
Then where the shore to the wide sea inclined
  I watched with new eyes the new sun's ascent:
  My heart was stirred within me as I leant
  And listened to a voice in every wind.
O purple sea! O joy beyond control!
  O land of love and youth! O happy throng!
  Were ye then real, or did ye only seem?
Dear is that morning twilight of the soul,—
  The mystery, the waking voice of song,—
  For now I know it was not all a dream.

## CONGRESS: 1878.

'Twas in the year when mutterings, loud and deep,
  From the roused beast were heard in all the land,
  And grave men questioned: "Can the State withstand
  The shock and strain to come? Oh, will she keep
Firm her four walls, should the wild creature leap
  To ruin and ravish? Will her pillars planned
  By the great dead, lean then to either hand?
  The dead! would heaven they might awake from
      sleep!"
Haply (I thought), our Congress still may hold
  One voice of power,— when lo! upon the blast
  A sound like jackals ravening to and fro.
Great God! And has it come to this at last?
  Such noise, such shame, where once, not long ago,
  The pure and wise their living thoughts outrolled.

## A PORTRAIT OF SERVETUS.

THOU grim and haggard wanderer who dost look
With haunting eyes forth from the narrow page,—
I know what fires consumed with inward rage
Thy broken frame, what tempests chilled and shook!
Ah, could not thy remorseless foeman brook
Time's sure devourment, but must needs assuage
His anger in thy blood, and blot the age
With that dark crime which virtue's semblance took!
Servetus! that which slew thee lives to-day,
Though in new forms it taints our modern air;
Still in heaven's name the deeds of hell are done:
Still on the high-road, 'neath the noon-day sun,
The fires of hate are lit for them who dare
Follow their Lord along the untrodden way.

## MODJESKA.

THERE are four sisters known to mortals well,
Whose names are Joy and Sorrow, Death and Love:
This last it was who did my footsteps move
To where the other deep-eyed sisters dwell.
To-night, or ere yon painted curtain fell,
These, one by one, before my eyes did rove
Through the brave mimic world that Shakespeare wove.
Lady! thy art, thy passion were the spell
That held me, and still holds; for thou dost show,
With those most high each in his sovereign art,—
Shakespeare supreme, and mighty Angelo,—
Great art and passion are one. Thine too the part
To prove, that still for him the laurels grow
Who reaches through the mind to pluck the heart.

## KEATS.

Touch not with dark regret his perfect fame,
  Sighing, "Had he but lived he had done so;"
  Or, "Were his heart not eaten out with woe
  John Keats had won a prouder, mightier name!"
Take him for what he was and did—nor blame
  Blind fate for all he suffered. Thou shouldst know
  Souls such as his escape no mortal blow—
  No agony of joy, or sorrow, or shame!
"Whose name was writ in water!" What large laughter
  Among the immortals when that word was brought!
  Then when his fiery spirit rose flaming after
High toward the topmost heaven of heavens up-caught!
  "All hail! our younger brother!" Shakespeare said,
  And Dante nodded his imperial head.

## AN INSCRIPTION IN ROME.

(Piazza di Spagna.)

Something there is in Death not all unkind,
He hath a gentler aspect, looking back;
For flowers may bloom in the dread thunder's track,
And even the cloud that struck with light was lined.
Thus, when the heart is silent, speaks the mind;
But there are moments when comes rushing, black
And fierce upon us, the old, awful lack,
And Death once more is cruel, senseless, blind.
So when I saw beside a Roman portal
"In this house died John Keats"—for tears that sprung
I could no further read. O bard immortal!
Not for thy fame's sake—but so young, so young;
Such beauty vanished, spilled such heavenly wine,
All quenched that power of deathless song divine!

## "CALL ME NOT DEAD."

CALL me not dead when I, indeed, have gone
  Into the company of the everliving
  High and most glorious poets! Let thanksgiving
  Rather be made. Say—"He at last hath won
Rest and release, converse supreme and wise,
  Music and song and light of immortal faces:
  To-day, perhaps, wandering in starry places,
  He hath met Keats, and known him by his eyes.
To-morrow (who can say) Shakespeare may pass,—
  And our lost friend just catch one syllable
  Of that three-centuried wit that kept so well,—
Or Milton,—or Dante, looking on the grass
  Thinking of Beatrice, and listening still
  To chanted hymns that sound from the heavenly hill."

## TO A DEPARTED FRIEND.

DEAR friend, who lovedst well this pleasant life!
  One year ago it is this very day
  Since thou didst take thy uncompanioned way
  Into the silent land, from out the strife
And joyful tumult of the world. The knife
  Wherewith that sorrow smote us, still doth stay,
  And we, to whom thou daily didst betray
  Thy gentle soul, with faith and worship rife,
Love thee not less but more,—as time doth go
  And we too hasten toward that land unknown
  Where those most dear are gathering one by one.
The power divine that here did touch thy heart—
  Hath this withdrawn from thee, where now thou art?
  Would thou indeed couldst tell what thou dost know.

## "H. H."

I WOULD that in the verse she loved some word,
Not all unfit, I to her praise could frame:
Some word wherein the memory of her name
Might through long years its incense still afford.
But no, her spirit smote with its own sword;
Herself has lit the fire whose blood-red flame
Shall not be quenched: this is her living fame
Who struck so well the sonnet's subtle chord.
None who e'er knew her can believe her dead;
Though should she die they deem it well might be
Her spirit took its everlasting flight
In summer's glory, by the sunset sea,—
That onward through the Golden Gate it fled.
Ah, where that bright soul is cannot be night.

## LOVE AND DEATH.

I.

Now who can take from us what we have known—
 We that have looked into each other's eyes?
 Though sudden night should blacken all the skies,
 The day is ours, and what the day has shown.
What we have seen and been, hath not this grown
 Part of our very selves? We, made love-wise,
 What power shall slay our living memories,
 And who shall take from us what is our own?
So, when a shade of the last parting fell,
 This thought gave peace, as he deep comfort hath
 Who, thirsting, drinks cool waters from a well.
But soon I felt more near that fatal breath:
 More near he drew, till I his face could tell,
 Till then unseen, unknown,—I looked on Death.

II.

We know not where they tarry who have died;
The gate wherein they entered is made fast:
No living mortal hath seen one who passed
Hither, from out that darkness deep and wide.
We lean on Faith; and some less wise have cried,
"Behold the butterfly, the seed that 's cast!"
Vain hopes that fall like flowers before the blast!
What man can look on Death unterrified?——
Who love can never die! They are a part
Of all that lives beneath the summer sky;
With the world's living soul their souls are one:
Nor shall they in vast nature be undone
And lost in the general life. Each separate heart
Shall live, and find its own, and never die.

## "THE EVENING STAR."

THE evening star trembles and hides from him
  Who fain would hold it with imperious stare;
  Yet, to the averted eye, lo! unaware
  It shines serene, no longer shy and dim.
Oh, slow and sweet, its chalice to the brim
  Fills the leaf-shadowed grape with rich and rare
  Cool sunshine, caught from the white circling air!
  Home from his journey to the round world's rim—
Through lonely lands, through cloudy seas and vext—
  At last the Holy Grail met Launfal's sight.
  So when my friend lost him who was her next
Of soul,—life of her life,—all day the fight
  Raged with a dumb and pitiless God. Perplexed
  She slept. Heaven sent its comfort in the night.

## COST.

BECAUSE Heaven's cost is Hell, and perfect joy
  Hurts as hurts sorrow; and because we win
  No boon of grace without the cost of sin,
  Or suffering born of sin; because the alloy
Of blood but makes the bliss of victory brighter;
  Because true worth hath its sure proof herein—
  That it should be reproached, and called akin
  To evil things,—black making white the whiter:
Because no cost seems great near this—that He
  Should pay the ransom wherewith we were priced;
  And none could name a darker infamy
Than that a God was spit upon—enticed
  By those he came to save, to the accursèd tree—
  For this I know that Christ indeed is Christ.

## "DAY UNTO DAY UTTERETH SPEECH."

THE speech that day doth utter, and the night,
Full oft to mortal ears it hath no sound;
Dull are our eyes to read upon the ground
What's written there; and stars are hid by light.
So when the dark doth fall, awhile our sight
Kens the unwonted orbs that circle round,
Then quick in sleep our human sense is bound:
Speechless for us the starry heavens and bright.
But when the day doth close there is one word
That's writ amid the sunset's golden embers;
And one at morn; by them our hearts are stirred:
Splendor of Dawn,—and Evening that remembers;
These are the rhymes of God; thus, line on line,
Our souls are moved to thoughts that are divine.

## FATHER AND CHILD.

Beneath the deep and solemn midnight sky,
At this last verge and boundary of time
I stand, and listen to the starry chime
That sounds to the inward sense, and will not die.
Now do the thoughts that daily hidden lie
Arise, and live in a celestial clime,—
Unutterable thoughts, most high, sublime,
Crossed by one dread that frights mortality.
Thus, as I muse, I hear my little child
Sob in its sleep within the cottage near,—
My own dear child! — Gone is that mortal doubt!
The Power that drew our lives forth from the wild
Our Father is; we shall to him be dear,
Nor from his universe be blotted out!

## THE CELESTIAL PASSION.

O WHITE and midnight sky, O starry bath,
  Wash me in thy pure, heavenly, crystal flood:
  Cleanse me, ye stars, from earthly soil and scath —
  Let not one taint remain in spirit or blood!
Receive my soul, ye burning, awful deeps,
  Touch and baptize me with the mighty power
  That in ye thrills, while the dark planet sleeps;
  Make me all thine for one blest, secret hour!
O glittering host, O high angelic choir,
  Silence each tone that with thy music jars;
  Fill me even as an urn with thy white fire
Till all I am is kindred to the stars!
  Make me thy child, thou infinite, holy night,—
  So shall my days be full of heavenly light!

# ODES AND MEDITATIVE POEMS.

# MUSIC AND WORDS.

I.

THIS day I heard such music that I thought:
Hath human speech the power thus to be wrought,
Into such melody; pure, sensuous sound,—
Into such mellow, murmuring mazes caught;
Can words (I said), when these keen tones are bound —
(Silent, except in memory of this hour)—
Can human words alone usurp the power
Of trembling strings that thrill to the very soul,
And of this ecstasy bring back the whole?

II.

Ah no, 'twas answered in my inmost heart,
Unto itself sufficient is each art,
And each doth utter what none other can —
Some hidden mood of the large soul of man.

Ah, think not thou with words well interweaved
To wake the tones wherein the viol grieved
With its most heavy burden; think not thou,
Adventurous, to push thy shallop's prow
Into that surge of well-remembered tones,—
Striving to match each wandering wind that moans,
Each bell that tolls, and every bugle's blowing
With some most fitting word, some verse bestowing
A never-shifting form on that which passed
Swift as a bird that glimmers down the blast.

III.

So, still unworded, save in memory mute,
Rest thou sweet hour of viol and of lute;
Of thoughts that never, never can be spoken,
Too frail for the rough usage of men's words,—
Thoughts that shall keep their silence all unbroken
Till music once more stirs them:—then like birds
That in the night-time slumber, they shall wake,
While all the leaves of all the forest shake;—
Oh, hark, I hear it now that tender strain
Fulfilled with all of sorrow save its pain.

## THE POET'S FAME.

MANY the songs of power the poet wrought
To shake the hearts of men. Yea, he had caught
The inarticulate and murmuring sound
That comes at midnight from the darkened ground
When the earth sleeps; for this he framed a word
Of human speech, and hearts were strangely stirred
That listened. And for him the evening dew
Fell with a sound of music, and the blue
Of the deep, starry sky he had the art
To put in language that did seem a part
Of the great scope and progeny of nature.
In woods, or waves, or winds, there was no creature
Mysterious to him. He was too wise
Either to fear, or follow, or despise
Whom men call Science,—for he knew full well
All she had told, or still might live to tell,
Was known to him before her very birth:

Yea, that there was no secret of the earth,
Nor of the waters under, nor the skies,
That had been hidden from the poet's eyes;
By him there was no ocean unexplored,
Nor any savage coast that had not roared
Its music in his ears.

He loved the town,—
Not less he loved the ever-deepening brown
Of summer twilights on the enchanted hills;
Where he might listen to the starts and thrills
Of birds that sang and rustled in the trees,
Or watch the footsteps of the wandering breeze
And the birds' shadows as they fluttered by
Or slowly wheeled across the unclouded sky.
All these were written on the poet's soul,—
But he knew, too, the utmost, distant goal
Of the human mind. His fiery thought did run
To Time's beginning, ere yon central sun
Had warmed to life the swarming broods of men.
In waking dreams, his many-visioned ken
Clutched the large, final destiny of things.

He heard the starry music, and the wings
Of beings unfelt by others thrilled the air
About him. Yet the loud and angry blare
Of tempests found an echo in his verse,
And it was here that lovers did rehearse
The ditties they would sing when, not too soon,
Came the warm night,—shadows, and stars, and moon.
Who heard his songs were filled with noble rage,
And wars took fire from his prophetic page:
Most righteous wars, wherein, 'midst blood and tears,
The world rushed onward through a thousand years.
And still he made the gentle sounds of peace
Heroic,—bade the nation's anger cease!
Bitter his songs of grief for those who fell,—
And for all this the people loved him well.

They loved him well and therefore, on a day,
They said with one accord: "Behold how gray
Our poet's head hath grown! Ere 't is too late
Come, let us crown him in our Hall of State:
Ring loud the bells, give to the winds his praise,
And urge his fame to other lands and days!"

So was it done, and deep his joy therein.
But passing home at night, from out the din
Of the loud Hall, the poet, unaware,
Moved through a lonely and dim-lighted square—
There was the smell of lilacs in the air
And then the sudden singing of a bird,
Startled by his slow tread. What memory stirred
Within his brain he told not. Yet this night—
Lone lingering when the eastern heavens were bright—
He wove a song of such immortal art
That there is not in all the world one heart—
One human heart unmoved by it. Long! long!
The laurel-crown has failed, but not that song
Born of the night and sorrow. Where he lies
At rest beneath the ever-shifting skies,
Age after age, from far-off lands they come,
With tears and flowers, to seek the poet's tomb.

## THE POET AND HIS MASTER.

ONE day the poet's harp lay on the ground,
Though from it rose a strange and trembling sound
What time the wind swept over with a moan,
Or, now and then, a faint and tinkling tone
When a dead leaf fell shuddering from a tree
And shook the silent wires all tremulously;
And near it, solemn-eyed and woe-begone,
The poet sat: he did not weep or groan.

Then one drew near him who was robed in white:
It was the poet's master; he had given
To him that harp, once in a happy night
When every silver star that shone in heaven
Made music ne'er before was heard by mortal wight.
And thus the master spoke:

"Why is thy voice
Silent, O poet? Why upon the grass
Lies thy still harp? The fitful breezes pass
And touch the wires, but the skilled player's hand
Moves not upon them. Poet,—wake! Rejoice,
Sing and arouse the melancholy land."

"Master, forbear. I may not sing to-day:
My nearest friend, the brother of my heart,
This day is stricken with sorrow, he must part
From her who loves him. Can I sing, and play
Upon the joyous harp, and mock his woe?"

"Alas, and hast thou then so soon forgot
The bond that with thy gift of song did go—
Severe as fate, fixed and unchangeable?
Dost thou not know this is the poet's lot:
'Mid sounds of war—in halcyon times of peace—
To strike the ringing wire and not to cease;
In hours of general happiness to swell
The common joy; and when the people cry
With piteous voice loud to the pitiless sky,

'Tis his to frame the universal prayer,
And breathe the balm of song upon the accursèd air?"

"But 'tis not, O my master, that I borrow
The robe of grief to deck my brother's sorrow,—
Mine eyes have seen beyond the veil of youth;
I know what Life is, have caught sight of Truth;
My heart is dead within me; a thick pall
Darkens the mid-day sun."

"And dost thou call
This sorrow? Call this knowledge? O thou blind
And ignorant! Know, then, thou yet shalt find,
Ere thy full days are numbered 'neath the sun,
Thou, in thy shallow youth, hadst but begun
To guess what knowledge is, what grief may be,
And all the infinite sum of human misery;
Shalt find that for each drop of perfect good
Thou payest, at last, a threefold price in blood;
What is most noble in thee,—every thought
Highest and best,—crushed, spat upon, and brought
To open shame; thy natural ignorance

Counted thy crime; the world all ruled by chance,
Save that the good most suffer; but above
These ills another,—cruel, monstrous, worse
Than all before,—thy pure and passionate love
Shall bring the old, immitigable curse."

"And thou who tell'st me this, dost bid me sing?"

"I bid thee sing, even though I have not told
All the deep flood of anguish shall be rolled
Across thy breast. Nor, Poet, shalt thou bring
From out those depths thy grief! Tell to the wind
Thy private woes, but not to human ear,
Save in the shape of comfort for thy kind.
But never hush thy song, dare not to cease
While life is thine. Haply, 'mid those who hear,
Thy music to one soul shall murmur peace,
Though for thyself it hath no power to cheer.

"Then shall thy still unbroken spirit grow
Strong in its silent suffering and more wise;
And as the drenched and thunder-shaken skies

Pass into golden sunset — thou shalt know
An end of calm, when evening breezes blow;
And looking on thy life with vision fine
Shalt see the shadow of a hand divine."

## ODE.

I AM the spirit of the morning sea;
I am the awakening and the glad surprise;
I fill the skies
With laughter and with light.
Not tears, but jollity
At birth of day brim the strong man-child's eyes.
Behold the white
Wide three-fold beams that from the hidden sun
Rise swift and far,—
One where Orion keeps
His armèd watch, and one
That to the midmost starry heaven upleaps;
The third blots out the firm-fixed Northern Star.
  I am the wind that shakes the glittering wave,
Hurries the snowy spume along the shore

And dies at last in some far-murmuring cave.
My voice thou hearest in the breaker's roar,—
That sound which never failed since time began,
And first around the world the shining tumult ran.

II.

I light the sea and wake the sleeping land.
My footsteps on the hills make music, and my hand
Plays like a harper's on the wind-swept pines.

With the wind and the day
I follow round the world—away! away!
Wide over lake and plain my sunlight shines
And every wave and every blade of grass
Doth know me as I pass;
And me the western sloping mountains know, and me
The far-off, golden sea.

O sea, whereon the passing sun doth lie!
O man, who watchest by that golden sea!
Weep not,—O weep not thou, but lift thine eye
And see me glorious in the sunset sky!

III.

I love not the night
Save when the stars are bright,
Or when the moon
Fills the white air with silence like a tune.
Yea, even the night is mine
When the Northern Lights outshine,
And all the wild heavens throb in ecstasy divine;—
Yea, mine deep midnight, though the black sky lowers,
When the sea burns white and breaks on the shore
in starry showers.

IV.

I am the laughter of the new-born child
On whose soft-breathing sleep an angel smiled.
And I all sweet first things that are:
First songs of birds, not perfect as at last,—
Broken and incomplete,—
But sweet, oh, sweet!
And I the first faint glimmer of a star
To the wrecked ship that tells the storm is past;
The first keen smells and stirrings of the Spring;

First snow-flakes, and first May-flowers after snow;
The silver glow
Of the new moon's ethereal ring;
The song the morning stars together made,
And the first kiss of lovers under the first June shade.

V.

My sword is quick, my arm is strong to smite
In the dread joy and fury of the fight.
I am with those who win, not those who fly;
With those who live I am, not those who die.
Who die? Nay—nay—that word
Where I am is unheard;
For I am the spirit of youth that cannot change,
Nor cease, nor suffer woe;
And I am the spirit of beauty that doth range
Through natural forms and motions, and each show
Of outward loveliness. With me have birth
All gentleness and joy in all the earth.
Raphael knew me, and showed the world my face;
Me Homer knew, and all the singing race,—
For I am the spirit of light, and life, and mirth.

## AT THE PRESIDENT'S GRAVE.

(SEPTEMBER 19, 1881.)

All summer long the people knelt
And listened at the sick man's door:
Each pang which that pale sufferer felt
Throbbed through the land from shore to shore;

And as the all-dreaded hour drew nigh,
What breathless watching, night and day!
What tears, what prayers! Great God on high,—
Have we forgotten how to pray!

O broken-hearted, widowed one,
Forgive us if we press too near!
Dead is our husband, father, son,—
For we are all one household here.

And not alone here by the sea,
And not in his own land alone,
Are tears of anguish shed with thee—
In this one loss the world is one.

And thou remember,—though relief
Come not till thine own day grow dim,—
That never, in this world of grief,
Was mortal ever mourned like him.

## EPITAPH.

A man not perfect, but of heart
So high, of such heroic rage,
That even his hopes became a part
Of earth's eternal heritage.

## THE BURIAL OF GRANT.

(NEW-YORK, AUGUST 8, 1885.)

I.

Ye living soldiers of the mighty war,
  Once more from roaring cannon and the drums
  And bugles blown at morn, the summons comes;
Forget the halting limb, each wound and scar:
    Once more your Captain calls to you;
    Come to his last review!

II.

And come ye, too, bright spirits of the dead,
  Ye who went heavenward from the embattled field;
  And ye whose harder fate it was to yield
Life from the loathful prison or anguished bed:
    Dear ghosts! come join your comrades here
    Beside this sacred bier.

III.

Nor be ye absent, ye immortal band,—
  Warriors of ages past, and our own age,—
  Who drew the sword for right, and not in rage,
Made war that peace might live in all the land,
    Nor ever struck one vengeful blow,
    But helped the fallen foe.

IV.

And fail not ye — but, ah, ye falter not —
  To join his army of the dead and living,
  Ye who once felt his might, and his forgiving:
Brothers, whom more in love than hate he smote
    For all his countrymen make room
    By our great hero's tomb!

V.

Come soldiers,— not to battle as of yore,
  But come to weep; ay, shed your noblest tears;
  For lo, the stubborn chief, who knew not fears,
Lies cold at last, ye shall not see him more.
    How long grim Death he fought and well,
    That poor, lean frame doth tell.

VI.

All's over now; here let our Captain rest,
Silent amid the blare of praise and blame;
Here let him rest, alone with his great fame,—
Here in the city's heart he loved the best,
And where our sons his tomb may see
To make them brave as he:—

VII.

As brave as he—he on whose iron arm
Our Greatest leaned, our gentlest and most wise,—
Leaned when all other help seemed mocking lies,
While this one soldier checked the tide of harm,
And they together saved the State,
And made it free and great.

# A LAMENT

FOR THE DEAD OF THE "JEANNETTE" BROUGHT HOME ON THE "FRISIA."

I.

O GATES of ice! long have ye held our loved ones.

Ye Cruel! how could ye keep from us them for whom our hearts yearned: our dear ones, our fathers, our children, our brothers, our lovers.

Cold and Sleet, Darkness and Ice! hard have ye held them; ye would not let them go.

Their hands ye have bound fast; their feet ye have detained; and well have ye laid hold upon the hearts of our loved ones.

O silent Arctic Night! thou hast wooed them from us.

O Secret of the white and unknown world! too strong hast thou been for us; we were as nothing to thee; thou hast drawn them from us; thou wouldst not let them go.

The long day passed; thou wouldst not let them go.

The long, long night came and went; thou wouldst not let them go.

O thou insatiate! What to thee are youth, and life, and hope, and love?

For thou art Death, not Life; thou art Despair, not Hope.

Nought to thee the rush of youthful blood; nought to thee the beauty and strength of our loved ones.

The breath of their bodies was not sweet to thee; they loved thee, and thou lovedst not them.

They followed thee, thou didst not look upon them; but still, O thou inviolate! still did they follow thee.

Thee did they follow through storm, through perils of the ice, and of the unknown darkness.

The sharp spears of the frost they feared not; the terrors of death they feared not. For thee, for thee, for thee, not for us; only that they might look upon thy face!

All these they endured for thee; the thought of us whom yet they loved, this also they endured for thee.

For thou art beautiful, beyond the beauty of woman. In thy hair are the stars of night. Thou wrappest about thee garments of fire that burn not, and are never quenched;

When thou movest they are moved; when thou breathest they tremble.

Yea, awful art thou in thy beauty; with white fingers beckoning in mists and shadows of the frozen sea: drawing to thee the hearts of heroes.

II.

LONG, long have they tarried in thy gates, O North!

But now thou hast given them up. Lo, they come to us once more,—our beloved, our only ones!

O dearest, why have ye stayed so long?

With ye, night and day have come and gone, but with us there was night only.

But no, we will not reproach ye, hearts of our hearts,—dearest and best; our fathers, our children, our brothers, our lovers!

Come back to us! Behold our arms are open for you; ye are ours; ye have returned unto us; ye shall never go hence again.

But why are ye silent, why do ye not stir, why do ye not speak to us, O beloved ones?

White are your cheeks like snow; your eyes they do not look upon us.

So long ye have been gone, and is this your joy to see us once more?

Lo! do we not welcome you? Are not our souls glad? Do not our tears, long kept, fall upon your faces?

Or do ye but sleep well, after those hard and weary labors? O now awaken, for ye shall take rest and pleasure,— here are your homes and kindred!

Listen, beloved: here is your sister, here is your brother, here is your lover!

III.

THEY will not hearken to our voices.

They are still: their eyes look not upon us.

O insatiate, O Secret of the white and unknown world, cruel indeed thou art!

Thou hast sent back to us our best beloved; their bodies thou hast rendered up, but their spirits thou hast taken away from us forever.

In life thou didst hold them from us — and in death, in death they are thine.

NEW YORK, February 20, 1884.

## A THOUGHT.

ONCE, looking from a window on a land
That lay in silence underneath the sun:
A land of broad, green meadows, through which poured
Two rivers, slowly widening to the sea,—
Thus, as I looked, I know not how or whence,
Was borne into my unexpectant soul
That thought, late learned by anxious-witted man,
The infinite patience of the Eternal Mind.

## ILL TIDINGS.

(THE STUDIO CONCERT.)

In the long studio from whose towering walls
Greek Pheidias beams, and Angelo appalls,
Eager the listening, downcast faces throng
While violins their piercing tones prolong.
At times I know not if I see, or hear,
Milo's calm smile, or some not sorrowing tear
Down-falling on the surface of the stream
That music pours across my waking dream.
Ah, is it then a dream that while repeat
Those chords, like strokes of silver-shod light feet,
And the great Master's music marches on —
I hear the horses of the Parthenon?

. . . . .

But all to-day seems vague, unreal, far,
With fear and discord in the dearest strain,
For 'neath yon slowly-sinking western star
One that I love lies on her bed of pain.

## A NEW WORLD.

"I KNOW," he said,
"The thunder and the lightning have passed by
And all the earth is black, and burnt, and dead;
But, friend, the grass will grow again, the flowers
Again will bloom, the summer birds will sing,
And the all-healing sun will shine once more."
"Blind prophecy," she answered in her woe.
Yet still, as time wore on, the prophet's words
Came true,—but not all true. (So will it be
With all who here shall suffer mortal loss:)
Ere long the grass, the flowers, the birds, the sun
Once more made bright the bleak and desolate earth;
They came once more, those joys of other days;
She felt them, moved among them, and was glad.
Glad — glad! O mocking word! They came once more,
But not the same to her. Familiar they
As a remembered dream, and beautiful —
But changed, all changed, the whole world changed forever.

## FATE.

I flung a stone into a grassy field:
How many tiny creatures there may yield
(I thought) their petty lives through that rude shock!
To me a pebble, 'tis to them a rock,
Gigantic, cruel, fraught with sudden death.
Perhaps it crushed an ant, perhaps its breath
Alone tore down a white and glittering palace,
And the small spider damns the giant's malice
Who wrought the wreck — blasted his pretty art!

Who knows what day some saunterer, light of heart,
An idle wanderer through the fields of space,
Large-limbed, big-brained, to whom our puny race
Seem small as insects,— one whose footstep jars
On some vast continent islanded by stars,—
May fling a stone and crush our earth to bits,
And all that men have builded by their wits?

"Ah, what a loss!" you say; "our bodies go,
But not our temples, statues, and the glow
Of glorious canvases; and not the pages
Our poets have illumed through myriad ages.
What boots the insect's loss? Another day
Will see the self-same ant-hill and the play
Of light on dainty web the same. But blot
All human art from this terrestrial plot,
Something indeed would pass that nevermore
Would light the universe as once before!"
The spider's work is not original,—
You say,—but what of ours? I fear that all
We do is just the same thing over and over.
Take Life: you have the woman and her lover,—
'Tis old as Eden,—nought is new in that!
Take Building, and you reach ere long the flat
Nile desert sands, by way of France, Rome,
Greece.
And there is poetry—our bards increase
In numbers, not in sweetness, not in force
Since Job with the Eternal held discourse.
No, no! The forms may change, but even they

Come round again. Could we but truly scan it,
We'd find in the heavens some little, busy planet
Whence all we are was borrowed. If to-day
The imagined giant flung his ponderous stone,
And we and all our far-stretched schemes were done,
His were a scant remorse and short-lived trouble,—
Like mine for those small creatures in the stubble.

## THE VOICE OF THE PINE.

'Tis night upon the lake. Our bed of boughs
Is built where — high above — the pine-tree soughs.
'Tis still,—and yet what woody noises loom
Against the background of the silent gloom!
One well might hear the opening of a flower
If day were hushed as this. A mimic shower
Just shaken from a branch, how large it sounded,
As 'gainst our canvas roof its three drops bounded!
Across the rumpling waves the hoot-owl's bark
Tolls forth the midnight hour upon the dark.
What mellow booming from the hills doth come?—
The mountain quarry strikes its mighty drum.

Long had we lain beside our pine-wood fire,
From things of sport our talk had risen higher;
How frank and intimate the words of men
When tented lonely in some forest glen!

No dallying now with masks, from whence emerges
Scarce one true feature forth. The night-wind urges
To straight and simple speech. So we had thought
Aloud; no well-hid secrets but were brought
To light. The spiritual hopes, the wild,
Unreasoned longings that, from child to child,
Mortals still cherish (though with modern shame),—
To these, and things like these, we gave a name;
And as we talked, the intense and resinous fire
Lit up the towering boles, till nigh and nigher
They gathered round, a ghostly company,
Like beasts who seek to know what men may be.

Then to our hemlock beds, but not to sleep,—
For listening to the stealthy steps that creep
About the tent, or falling branch, but most
A noise was like the rustling of a host,
Or like the sea that breaks upon the shore,—
It was the pine-tree's murmur. More and more
It took a human sound. These words I felt
Into the skyey darkness float and melt:

"Heardst thou these wanderers reasoning of a time
When men more near the Eternal One shall climb?
How like the new-born child, who cannot tell
A mother's arm that wraps it warm and well!
Leaves of His rose; drops in His sea that flow,—
Are they, alas, so blind they cannot know
Here, in this breathing world of joy and fear,
They can no nearer get to God than here."

## THE HOMESTEAD.

### I.

HERE stays the house, here stay the self-same places,
Here the white lilacs and the buttonwoods;
Here are the pine-groves, there the river-floods,
And there the threading brook that interlaces
Green meadow-bank with meadow-bank the same.
The melancholy nightly chorus came
Long, long ago from the same pool, and yonder
Stark poplars lift in the same twilight air
Their ancient shadows: nearer still, and fonder,
The black-heart cherry-tree's gaunt branches bare
Rasp on the same old window where I ponder.

II.

And we, the only living, only pass;
We come and go, whither and whence we know not:
From birth to bound the same house keeps, alas!
New lives as gently as the old; there show not
Among the haunts that each had thought his own
The looks that parting brings to human faces.
The black-heart there, that heard my earliest moan,
And yet shall hear my last, like all these places
I love so well, unloving lives from child
To child; from morning joy to evening sorrow—
Untouched by joy, by anguish undefiled:
All one the generations gone, and new;
All one dark yesterday and bright to-morrow;
To the old tree's insensate sympathy
All one the morning and the evening dew—
My far, forgotten ancestor and I.

## "BEYOND THE BRANCHES OF THE PINE."

Beyond the branches of the pine
The golden sun no more doth shine,
  But still the solemn after-glow
Floods the deep heavens with light divine.

The night-wind stirs the corn-field near,
The gray moon turns to silver clear,
  And one by one the glimmering stars
In the blue dome of heaven appear.

Now do the mighty hosts of light
Across the darkness take their flight,—
  They rise above the eastern hill
And silent journey through the night.

And there beneath the starry zone,
In the deep, narrow grave, alone,
  Rests all that mortal was of her,
The purest spirit I have known.

## AN AUTUMN MEDITATION.

As THE long day of cloud and storm and sun
Declines into the dark and silent night,
So passed the old man's life from human gaze;
But not till sunset, full of lovely light
And color that the day might not reveal,
Bathed in soft gloom the landscape.

Thus kind Heaven
Let me, too, die when Autumn holds the year,
Serene, with tender hues, and bracing airs,—
And near me those I love; with no black thoughts,
Nor dread of what may come! Yea, when I die
Let me not miss from nature the cool rush
Of northern winds; let Autumn sunset skies
Be golden; let the cold, clear blue of night
Whiten with stars as now! Then shall I fade
From life to life,—pass on the year's full tide

Into the swell and vast of the outer sea
Beyond this narrow world.

For autumn days
To me not melancholy are, but full
Of joy and hope, mysterious and high,
And with strange promise rife. Then it meseems
Not failing is the year, but gathering fire
Even as the cold increases.

Grows a weed
More richly here beside our mellow seas
That is the Autumn's harbinger and pride.
When fades the cardinal-flower, whose heart-red bloom
Glows like a living coal upon the green
Of the midsummer meadows, then how bright,
How deepening bright like mounting flame doth burn
The golden-rod upon a thousand hills!
This is the Autumn's flower, and to my soul
A token fresh of beauty and of life,
And life's supreme delight.

When I am gone,
Something of me I would might subtly pass
Within these flowers twain of all the year:
So might my spirit send a sudden stir
Into the hearts of those who love these hills,
These woods, these waves, and meadows by the sea.

## RECOGNITION.

I.

In darkness of the visionary night
This I beheld: Wide space and therein God,
God who in dual nature doth abide,—
Love, and the Loved One, Power, and Beauty's self.
And forth from God did come, with dreadful thrill,
Creation, boundless, to the eye unformed,
And white with trembling fire and light intense,
And outward pulsings like the boreal flame;
One mighty cloud it seemed, nor star, nor earth,
Or like some nameless growth of the under-seas:
Creation dumb, unconscious, yet alive
With swift, concentric, never-ceasing urge,
Resolving gradual to one disk of fire.
And as I looked, behold the flying rim
Grew separate from the center; this again
Divided, and the whole still swift revolved,
Ring within ring, and fiery wheel in wheel;

Till, sudden or slow as chanced, the outmost edge
Whirled into fragments, each a separate sun,
With lesser globes attendant on its flight.
These while I gazed turned dark with smouldering fire
And, slow contracting, grew to solid orbs.
Then knew I that this planetary world,
Cradled in light, and curtained with the dawn
And starry eve, was born; though in itself
Complete and perfect all, yet but a part
And atom of the living universe.

II.

Unconscious still the child of the conscious God,—
Creation, born of Beauty and of Love,
Beauty the womb and mother of all worlds.
But soon with silent speed the new-made earth
Swept near me where I watched the birth of things,
Its greatening bulk eclipsing, star by star,
Half the bright heavens. Then I beheld crawl forth
Upon the earth's cool crust most wondrous forms
Wherein were hid, in transmutation strange,

Sparks of the ancient, never-ending fire;
Shapes moved not solely by exterior law
But having will and motion of their own,—
First sluggish and minute, then by degrees
Monstrous, enorm. Then other forms more fine
Streamed ceaseless on my sight, until at last,
Rising and turning its slow gaze about
Across the abysmal void the mighty child
Of the supreme, divine Omnipotence—
Creation, born of God, by Him begot,
Conscious in MAN, no longer blind and dumb,
Beheld and knew its father and its God.

# THE NEW DAY,

A POEM IN SONGS AND SONNETS.

# PRELUDE.

THE night was dark, though sometimes a faint star
A little while a little space made bright.
Dark was the night and like an iron bar
Lay heavy on the land: till o'er the sea
Slowly, within the East, there grew a light
Which half was starlight, and half seemed to be
The herald of a greater. The pale white
Turned slowly to pale rose, and up the height
Of heaven slowly climbed. The gray sea grew
Rose-colored like the sky. A white gull flew
Straight toward the utmost boundary of the East
Where slowly the rose gathered and increased.
It was as on the opening of a door
By one who in his hand a lamp doth hold,
(Its flame yet hidden by the garment's fold)—
The still air moves, the wide room is less dim.

More bright the East became, the ocean turned
Dark and more dark against the brightening sky—
Sharper against the sky the long sea line.
The hollows of the breakers on the shore
Were green like leaves whereon no sun doth shine,
Though white the outer branches of the tree.
From rose to red the level heaven burned;
Then sudden, as if a sword fell from on high,
A blade of gold flashed on the ocean's rim.

# PART I.

I.

## SONNET.

(AFTER THE ITALIAN.)

I KNOW not if I love her overmuch;
But this I know, that when unto her face
She lifts her hand, which rests there, still, a space,
Then slowly falls—'tis I who feel that touch.
And when she sudden shakes her head, with such
A look, I soon her secret meaning trace.
So when she runs I think 'tis I who race.
Like a poor cripple who has lost his crutch
I am if she is gone; and when she goes,
I know not why, for that is a strange art—
As if myself should from myself depart.
I know not if I love her more than those
Her lovers, but for the red hidden rose
She covers in her hair, I 'd give my heart.

## II.

## SONNET.

(AFTER THE ITALIAN.)

I LIKE her gentle hand that sometimes strays,
To find the place, through the same book with mine;
I like her feet; and oh, her eyes are fine!
And when we say farewell, perhaps she stays
Love-lingering—then hurries on her ways,
As if she thought, "To end my pain and thine."
I like her voice better than new-made wine,
I like the mandolin whereon she plays.
And I like, too, the cloak I saw her wear,
And the red scarf that her white neck doth cover,
And well I like the door that she comes through;
I like the riband that doth bind her hair,—
But then, in truth, I am that lady's lover,
And every new day there is something new.

III.

## "A BARREN STRETCH THAT SLANTS TO THE SALT SEA'S GRAY."

A BARREN stretch that slants to the salt sea's gray—
  Rock-strewn, and scarred by fire, and rough with
      stubble,—
With here and there a bold, bright touch of color
Berries and yellow leaves—that make the dolor
  More dolorous still. Above, a sky of trouble.

But now a light is lifted in the air;
  And though the sky is shadowed, fold on fold,
  By clouds that have the lightnings in their hold,
That western gleam makes all the dim earth fair—
  The sun shines forth and the gray sea is gold.

IV.

## LOVE IN WONDER.

(A PICTURE.)

TO-DAY I saw the picture of a man
  Who, issuing from a wood, doth thrust apart
  Strong-matted, thorny branches, whose keen smart
  He heeds in nowise, if he only can
Win the red rose a maiden, like a fan,
  Holds daintily. She, listening to her heart,
  Hath looked another way. Ah, would she start,
  And weep, and suffer sorrow, if he ran—
For utter love of her—swift, sobbing, back
  Into those awful shadows, terribler
  Because her whiteness made their black more black!
A little while he waits, lest he should err;
  Awhile he wonders, secretly.—Alack!
  He could so gladly die, or live for her.

V.

## LOVE GROWN BOLD.

THIS is her picture painted ere mine eyes
  Her ever holy face had looked upon.
  She sitteth in a silence of her own;
  Behind her, on the ground, a red rose lies:
Her thinking brow is bent, nor doth arise
  Her gaze from that shut book whose word unknown
  Her firm hands hide from her;—there all alone
  She sitteth in thought-trouble, maidenwise.
And now her lover waiting wondereth
  Whether the joy of joys is drawing near:
  Shall his brave fingers like a tender breath
That shut book open for her, wide and clear?
  From him who her sweet shadow worshippeth
  Now will she take the rose, and hold it dear?

INTERLUDE.

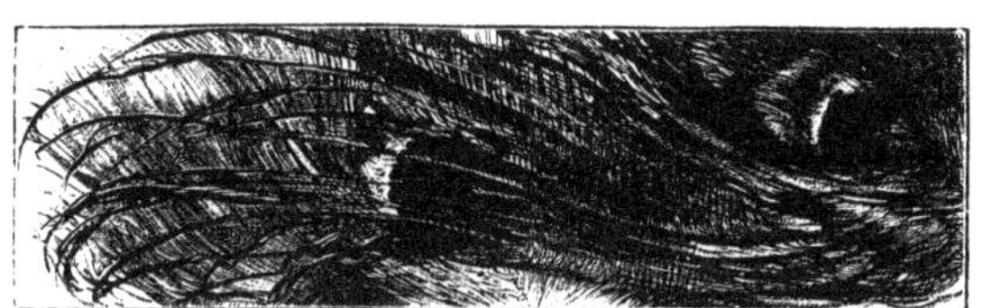

THE sun rose swift and sent a golden gleam
Across the moving waters to the land;
Then for a little while it seemed to stand
In a clear place, midway 'twixt sea and cloud;
Whence rising swift again it passed behind
Full many a long and narrow cloud-wrought beam
Encased in gold unearthly, that was mined
From out the hollow caverns of the wind.
These first revealed its face and next did shroud,
While still the daylight grew, and joy thereby
Lit all the windy stretches of the sky:

Until a shadow darkened from the east
And sprang upon the ocean like a beast.

# PART II.

## I.

THERE was a field green and fragrant with grass and flowers, and flooded with sunlight, and the air above it throbbed with the songs of birds. It was yet morning when sudden darkness came, and fire followed lightning over its face, and the singing birds fell dying upon the blackened grass. The thunder and the flame passed, but it was still dark,—till a ray of light touched the field's edge and grew, little by little. Then I who listened heard—not the songs of birds again, but the flutter of broken wings.

II.

## THE DARK ROOM.

(A PARABLE)

I.

A MAIDEN sought her love in a dark room,—
  So early had she yearned from yearning sleep,
  So hard it was from her true love to keep,—
  And blind she went through that all-silent gloom,
Like one who wanders weeping in a tomb.
  Heavy her heart, but her light fingers leap
  With restless grasp and question in that deep
  Unanswering void. Now when a hand did loom
At last, how swift her warm impassioned face
  Pressed 'gainst the black and solemn-yielding air,
  As near more near she groped to that bright place,
And seized the hand, and drowned it with her hair,
  And bent her body to his fierce embrace,
  And knew what joy was in the darkness there.

II.

GREAT GOD! the arms wherein that maiden fell
  Were not her lover's; I am her lover—I,
  Who sat here in the shadows silently—
  Silent with gladness, for I thought, O hell!
I thought to me she moved, and all was well.
  She saw me not, yet dimly could descry
  That beautiful hand of his, and with a sigh
  Sank on his fair and treacherous breast. The spell
Of the Evil One was on me. All in vain
  I strove to speak—my parchéd lips were dumb.
  See! see! the wan and whitening window-pane!
See, in the night, the awful morning bloom!
  Too late she will know all! Heaven! send thy rain
  Of death, nor let the sun of waking come!

III.

## I MET A TRAVELLER ON THE ROAD.

I MET a traveller on the road
Whose back was bent beneath a load;
His face was worn with mortal care,
His frame beneath its burden shook,
Yet onward, restless, he did fare
With mien unyielding, fixed, a look
Set forward in the empty air
As if he read an unseen book.
  What was it in his smile that stirred
My soul to pity! When I drew
More near it seemed as if I heard
The broken echo of a tune
Learned in some far and happy June.
His lips were parted, but unmoved
By words. He sang as dreamers do,
And not as if he heard and loved
The song he sang: I hear it now!

He stood beside the level brook,
Nor quenched his thirst, nor bathed his brow,
Nor from his back the burden shook.
He stood, and yet he did not rest;
His eyes climbed up in aimless quest,
Then close did to that mirror bow—
And, looking down, I saw in place
Of his, my own familiar face.

## IV.

## WRITTEN ON A FLY-LEAF OF "SHAKESPEARE'S SONNETS."

WHEN shall true love be love without alloy:
  Shine free at last from sinful circumstance!
  When shall the canker of unheavenly chance
  Eat not the bud of that most heavenly joy!
When shall true love meet love not as a coy
  Retreating light that leads a deathful dance,
  But as a firm fixed fire that doth enhance
  The beauty of all beauty! Will the employ
Of poets ever be too well to show
  That mightiest love with sharpest pain doth writhe;
  That underneath the fair, caressing glove
Hides evermore the iron hand; and though
  Love's flower alone is good, if we would prove
  Its perfect bloom, our breath slays like a scythe!

## V.

### "AND WERE THAT BEST!"

AND were that best, Love, dreamless, endless sleep!
  Gone all the fury of the mortal day;
  The daylight gone, and gone the starry ray!
  And were that best, Love, rest serene and deep!
Gone labor and desire; no arduous steep
  To climb, no songs to sing, no prayers to pray,
  No help for those who perish by the way,
  No laughter 'midst our tears, no tears to weep!
And were that best, Love, sleep with no dear dream,
  Nor memory of any thing in life—
  Stark death that neither help nor hurt can know!
Oh, rather, Love, the sorrow-bringing gleam,
  The living day's long agony and strife!
  Rather strong love in pain—the waking woe!

## VI.

## "THERE IS NOTHING NEW UNDER THE SUN."

THERE is nothing new under the sun;
  There is no new hope or despair;
The agony just begun
  Is as old as the earth and the air.
My secret soul of bliss
  Is one with the singing star's,
And the ancient mountains miss
  No hurt that my being mars.

I know as I know my life,
  I know as I know my pain,
That there is no lonely strife,
  That he is mad who would gain
A separate balm for his woe,
  A single pity and cover:
The one great God I know
  Hears the same prayer over and over.

I know it because at the portal
  Of Heaven I bowed and cried,
And I said, "Was ever a mortal
  Thus crowned and crucified!
My praise thou hast made my blame;
  My best thou hast made my worst;
My good thou hast turned to shame;
  My drink is a flaming thirst."

But scarce my prayer was said
  Ere from that place I turned;
I trembled, I hung my head,
  My cheek, shame-smitten, burned:
For there where I bowed down
  In my boastful agony,
I thought of thy cross and crown,—
  O Christ! I remembered thee.

## VII.

## LOVE'S CRUELTY.

"And this, then, is thy love," I hear thee say,
"And dost thou love, and canst thou torture so?
Ah, spare me, if thou lov'st me, this last woe!"
But I am not my own; I must obey
My master; I am slave to LOVE; his sway
Is cruel as the grave. When he says Go!
I go; when he says Come! I come. I know
No law but his. When he says Slay! I slay.
As cruel as the grave Yes—crueller.
Cruel as light that pours its stinging flood
Across the dark, and makes an anguished stir
Of life. Cruel as life that sends through blood
Of mortal the immortal pang and spur.
Cruel as thy remorseless maidenhood.

INTERLUDE.

THE cloud was thick that hid the sun from sight
And over all a shadowy roof outspread,
Making the day dim with another night—
Not dark like that which passed, but oh! more dread
For the clear sunlight that had gone before
And prophecy of that which yet should be.
Like snow at night the wind-blown hills of sand
Shone with an inward light far down the land:
Beneath the lowering sky black was the sea
Across whose waves a bird came flying low—
Borne swift on the wind with wing-beat halt and slow—
From out the dull east toward the foamy shore.
There was an awful waiting in the earth
As if a mystery greatened to its birth:
Though late it seemed, the day was just begun
When lo! at last, the many-colored bow
Stood in the heavens over against the sun.

# PART III.

I.

## "MY LOVE FOR THEE DOTH MARCH LIKE ARMED MEN."

My love for thee doth march like armèd men
  Against a queenly city they would take.
  Along the army's front its banners shake;
  Across the mountain and the sun-smit plain
It steadfast sweeps as sweeps the steadfast rain;
  And now the trumpet makes the still air quake,
  And now the thundering cannon doth awake
  Echo on echo, echoing loud again.
But, lo! the conquest higher than bard had sung;
  Instead of answering cannon comes a small
  White flag; the iron gates are open flung,
And flowers along the invaders' pathway fall.
  The city's conquerors feast their foes among,
  And their brave flags are trophies on her wall.

## II.

## "I WILL BE BRAVE FOR THEE."

I WILL be brave for thee, dear heart; for thee
My boasted bravery forego. I will
For thee be wise, or lose my little skill,—
Coward or brave; wise, foolish; bond or free.
No grievous cost in anything I see
That brings thee bliss, or only keeps thee, still,
In painless peace. So Heaven thy cup but fill,
Be empty mine unto eternity!
Come to me, Love, and let me touch thy face!
Lean to me, Love,—breathe on me thy dear breath!
Fly from me, Love, to some far hiding-place,
If thy one thought of me or hindereth
Or hurteth thy sweet soul—then grant me grace
To be forgotten, though that grace be death!

III.

## "LOVE ME NOT, LOVE, FOR THAT I FIRST LOVED THEE."

Love me not, Love, for that I first loved thee,
Nor love me, Love, for thy dear pity's sake,
In knowledge of the mortal pain and ache
Which is the fruit of love's blood-veinèd tree.
Let others for my love give love to me:
From other souls oh, gladly will I take,
This burning, heart-dry thirst of love to slake,
What seas of human pity there may be!
Nay, nay, I care no more how love may grow,
So that I hear thee answer to my call!
Love me because my piteous tears do flow,
Or that my love for thee did first befall.
Love me or late or early, fast or slow:
But love me, Love, for love is one and all!

IV.

## BODY AND SOUL.

I.

O THOU my Love, love first my lonely soul!
Then shall this too unworthy body of mine
Be loved by right and accident divine.
Forget the flesh, that the pure spirit's goal
May be the spirit; let that stand the whole
Of what thou lov'st in me. So will the shine
Of soul that strikes on soul make fair and fine
This earthy tenement. Thou shalt extol
The inner, that the outer lovelier seem.
Remember well that thy true love doth fear
No deadlier foe than the impassioned dream
Should drive thee to him, and should hold thee near—
Near to the body, not the soul of him.
Love first my soul and then both will be dear.

II.

BUT, Love, for me thy body was the first.
  One day I wandered idly through the town,
  Then entered a cathedral's silence brown
  Which sudden thrilled with a strange heavenly burst
Of light and music. Lo! that traveller durst
  Do nothing now but worship and fall down.
  He thought to rest, as doth some tired clown
  Who sinks in longed-for sleep, but there immersed
Finds restless vision on vision of beauty rare.
  Moved by thy body's outer majesty
  I entered in thy silent, sacred shrine:
'Twas then, all suddenly and unaware,
  Thou didst reveal, O maiden Love! to me,
  This beautiful, singing, holy soul of thine.

## V.

## "THY LOVER, LOVE, WOULD HAVE SOME NOBLER WAY."

THY lover, Love, would have some nobler way
  To tell his love, his noble love to tell,
  Than rhymes set ringing like a silver bell.
  Oh, he would lead an army, great and gay,
From conquering to conquer, day by day!
  And when the walls of a proud citadel
  At summons of his guns loud-echoing fell,—
  That thunder to his Love should murmuring say:
Thee only do I love, dear Love of mine!
  And while men cried: Behold how brave a fight!
  She should read well, oh well! each new emprise:
This to her lips, this to my lady's eyes!
  And though the world were conquered, line on line,
  Still would his love seem speechless, day and night.

VI.

## "WHAT WOULD I SAVE THEE FROM?"

WHAT would I save thee from, dear heart, dear heart?
Not from what Heaven may send thee of its pain;
Not from fierce sunshine or the scathing rain:
The pang of pleasure; passion's wound and smart;
Not from the scorn and sorrow of thine art;
Nor loss of faithful friends, nor any gain
Of growth by grief. I would not thee restrain
From needful death. But O, thou other part
Of me!—through whom the whole world I behold,
As through the blue I see the stars above!
In whom the world I find, hid fold on fold!
Thee would I save from this—nay, do not move!
Fear not, it may not flash, the air is cold;
Save thee from this—the lightning of my love.

## VII.

## LOVE'S JEALOUSY.

Of other men I know no jealousy,
  Nor of the maid who holds thee close, oh close!
  But of the June-red, summer-scented rose,
  And of the orange-streakéd sunset sky
That wins the soul of thee through thy deep eye;
  And of the breeze by thee beloved, that goes
  O'er thy dear hair and brow; the song that flows
  Into thy heart of hearts, where it may die.
I would I were one moment that sweet show
  Of flower; or breeze beloved that toucheth all;
  Or sky that through the summer eve doth burn.
I would I were the song thou lovest so,
  At sound of me to have thine eyelid fall:
  But I would then to something human turn.

## VIII.

## LOVE'S MONOTONE.

THOU art so used, Love, to thine own bird's song,—
  Sung to thine ear in love's low monotone,
  Sung to thee only, Love, to thee alone
  Of all the listening world,—that I among
My doubts find this the leader of the throng:
  Haply the music hath accustomed grown
  And no more music is to thee; my own
  Too faithful argument works its own wrong.
Ah Love, and must I learn for thy sweet sake
  The art of silence! Shut from me the light
  Of thy dear face then, lest the music wake!
Yet should thy bird at last fall silent quite,
  Would not thy heart an unused sorrow take?
  —Think not of me but of thyself to-night.

## IX.

## "ONCE ONLY."

ONCE only, Love, may love's sweet song be sung;
But once, Love, at our feet love's flower is flung;
Once, Love, once only, Love, can we be young:
    Say shall we love, dear Love, or shall we hate!

Once only, Love, will burn the blood-red fire;
But once awakeneth the wild desire;
Love pleadeth long, but what if Love should tire!
    Now shall we love, dear Love, or shall we wait!

The day is short, the evening cometh fast;
The time of choosing, Love, will soon be past;
The outer darkness falleth, Love, at last:
    Love, let us love ere it be late,—too late!

## X.

## DENIAL.

When some new thought of love in me is born
  Then swift I seek a token fair and meet
  That may unblamed thy blessed vision greet;
  Whether it be a rose, not bloodless torn
From that June tree which hideth many a thorn,
  Or but a simple, loving message, sweet
  With summer's heart and mine: these at thy feet
  I straightway fling—but all with maiden scorn
Thou spurnest. What to thee is token or sign,
  Who dost deny the thing wherefor it stands!
  Then I seem foolish in my sight and thine,
Like one who eager proffers empty hands.
  Thou only callest these my gifts unfine,
  While men are praising them in distant lands.

## XI.

## "ONCE WHEN WE WALKED WITHIN A SUMMER FIELD."

ONCE when we walked within a summer field
  I plucked the flower of immortality,
  And said, "Dear Love of mine, I give to thee
  This flower of flowers of all the round year's yield!"
'Twas then thou stood'st, and with one hand didst shield
  Thy sun-dazed eyes, and, flinging the other free,
  Spurned from thee that white blossom utterly.
  But, Love! the immortal can not so be killed.
The generations shall behold thee stand
  Against that western glow in grass dew-wet—
  Lord of my life, and lady of the land.
Nor maid nor lover shall the world forget,
  Nor that disdainful wafture of thy hand.
  Thou scornful! sun and flower shall find thee yet.

## XII.

## SONG.

I LOVE her gentle forehead,
  And I love her tender hair;
I love her cool, white arms,
  And her neck where it is bare.

I love the smell of her garments;
  I love the touch of her hands;
I love the sky above her,
  And the very ground where she stands.

I love her doubting and anguish;
  I love the love she withholds;
I love my love that loveth her
  And anew her being moulds.

## XIII.

## LISTENING TO MUSIC.

When on that joyful sea
Where billow on billow breaks; where swift waves follow
Waves, and hollow calls to hollow;
Where sea-birds swirl and swing.
And winds through the rigging shrill and sing;
Where night is night without a shade;
Where thy soul not afraid,
Though all alone unlonely,
Wanders and wavers, wavers wandering:—
On that accursèd sea
One moment only,
Forget one moment, Love, thy fierce content;
Back let thy soul be bent—
Think back, dear Love, O Love, think back to me!

XIV.

## "A SONG OF THE MAIDEN MORN."

A song of the maiden morn,
A song for my little maid,
Of the silver sunlight born!

But I am afraid, afraid,
When I come my maid may be
Nothing, there, but a shade.

But oh, her shadow is more to me
Than the shadowless light of eternity!

## XV.

## WORDS IN ABSENCE.

I WOULD that my words were as my fingers,
  So that my Love might feel them move
Slowly over her brow, as lingers
  The sunset wind o'er the world of its love.
I would that my words were as the beating
Of her own heart, that keeps repeating
  My name through the livelong day and the night;
And when my Love her lover misses—
  Longs for and loves in the dark and the light—
I would that my words were as my kisses.
I would that my words her life might fill,
  Be to her earth, and air, and skies.
I would that my words were hushed and still—
  Lost in the light of her eyes.

## XVI.

## SONG.

THE birds were singing, the skies were gay:
I looked from the window on meadow and wood,
On green, green grass that the sun made white;
Beyond the river the mountain stood,—
Blue was the mountain, the river was bright:
I looked on the land and it was not good,
For my own dear Love she had flown away.

## XVII.

## THISTLE-DOWN.

Fly, thistle-down, fly
From my lips to the lips that I love!
Fly through the morning light,
Flee through the shadowy night,
Over the sea and the land,
Quick as the lark
Through twilight and dark,
Through lightning and thunder;
Till no longer asunder
We stand;
For thy touch like the lips of her lover
Moves her being to mine,—
We are one in a swoon divine!

Fly, thistle-down, fly
From my lips to the lips that I love!

## XVIII.

## "O SWEET WILD ROSES THAT BUD AND BLOW."

O sweet wild roses that bud and blow
Along the way that my Love may go;
O moss-green rocks that touch her dress,
And grass that her dear feet may press;

O maple tree whose brooding shade
For her a summer tent has made;
O golden-rod and brave sun-flower
That flame before my maiden's bower;

O butterfly on whose light wings
The golden summer sunshine clings;
O birds that flit o'er wheat and wall,
And from cool hollows pipe and call;

O falling water whose distant roar
Sounds like the waves upon the shore;

O winds that down the valley sweep,
And lightnings from the clouds that leap;

O skies that bend above the hills,
O gentle rains and babbling rills,
O moon and sun that beam and burn—
Keep safe my Love till I return!

## XIX.

## THE RIVER.

I KNOW thou art not that brown mountain-side,
Nor the pale mist that lies along the hills
And with white joy the deepening valley fills;
Nor yet the solemn river moving wide
Into that valley, where the hills abide
But whence those morning clouds on noiseless wheels
Shall lingering lift and, as the moonlight steals
From out the heavens, so into the heavens shall glide.
I know thou art not this gray rock that looms
Above the water, fringed with scarlet vine;
Nor flame of burning meadow; nor the sedge
That sways and trembles at the river's edge.
But through all these, dear heart! to me there comes
Some melancholy, absent look of thine.

## XX.

## THE LOVER'S LORD AND MASTER.

I PRAY thee, dear, think not alone of me,
  But think sometimes of my great master, LOVE;
  His faithful slave he is so far above
  That for his sake I would forgotten be:
Though well I know that hidden thus from thee
  Not far away my image then might rove,
  And his sweet, heavenly countenance would move
  Ever thy soul to gentler charity:
So when thy lover's self leaps from his song,
  Thou him might love not less for his fair Lord.
  But that thy love for me grow never small
(As bow long bent twangs not the arrowed cord,
  And he doth lose his star who looks too long),
  Sometimes, dear heart, think not of me at all.

## XXI.

## "A NIGHT OF STARS AND DREAMS."

A NIGHT of stars and dreams, of dreams and sleep;
A waking into another empty day—
But not unlovely all, for then I say,
"To-morrow!" Through the hours this light doth creep
Higher in the heavens, as down the heavenly steep
Sinks the slow sun. Another evening gray,
Made glorious by the morn that comes that way;
Another night, and then To-day doth leap
Upon the world! Oh quick the hours do fly,
Of that new day which brings the moment when
We meet at last! Swift up the shaking sky
Rushes the sun from out its dismal den;
And then the wished for time doth yearn more nigh,
A white robe glimmering in the dark—and then!

## XXII.

## A BIRTHDAY SONG.

I THOUGHT this day to bring to thee
A flower that grows on the red rose tree.
I searched the branches,—oh, despair!
Of roses every branch was bare.

I thought to sing thee a birthday song
As wild as my love, as deep and strong.
The song took wing like a frightened bird,
And its music my maiden never heard.

But, Love! the flower and the song divine
One day of the year shall yet be thine;
And thou shalt be glad when the rose I bring,
And weep for joy at the song I sing.

## XXIII.

## "WHAT CAN LOVE DO FOR THEE, LOVE?"

WHAT can love do for thee, Love?
Can it make the green fields greener;
Bluer the skies, and bluer
The eyes of the blue-eyed flowers?
Can it make the May-day showers
More warm and sweet; serener
The heavens after the rain?
The sunset's radiant splendor
More exquisite and tender—
The Northern Star more sure?
Can it take the pang from pain?
(O Love! remember the curtain
Of cloud that lifted last night
And showed the silver light
Of a star!) Can it make more certain
The heart of the heart of all—

The good that works at the root—
The singing soul of love
That throbs in flower and fruit,
In man and earth and brute,
In hell, and heaven above?
Can its low voice musical
Make dear the day and the night?

## XXIV.

## FRANCESCA AND PAOLO.

WITHIN the second dolorous circle where
The lost are whirled, lamenting—thou and I
Stood, Love, to-day with Dante. Silently
We looked upon the black and trembling air:
When lo! from out that darkness of despair
Two shadows light upon the wind drew nigh,
Whose very motion seemed to breathe a sigh:
And there Francesca, and her lover there.
These when we saw, the wounds whereat they bled,
Their love which was not with their bodies slain—
These when we saw, great were the tears we shed:
As, Love, for thee and me love's tears shall rain—
The mortal agony, the nameless dread;
The longing, and the passion, and the pain.

## XXV.

## THE UNKNOWN WAY.

Two travellers met upon a plain
Where two straight, narrow pathways crossed;
They met and, with a still surprise,
They looked into each other's eyes
And knew that never, oh, never again!
Could one from the other soul be lost.

But lo! these narrow pathways lead
Now each from each apart, and lo!
In neither pathway can they go
Together, in their new, strange need.

Far-off the purple mountains loom—
Vague and far-off, and fixed as fate—
Which hide from sight that land unknown
Where, ever, like a carven stone
The setting sun doth stand and wait,

And men cry not, "Too late! too late!"
And sorrow turns to a golden gloom.

But oh, the long journey all unled
By track of traveller o'er the plain—
The stony desert, bleak and rude,
The bruiséd feet and the tired brain:
And oh, the two-fold solitude,
The doubt, the danger and the dread!

## XXVI.

## THE SOWER.

### I.

A Sower went forth to sow,
His eyes were dark with woe;
He crushed the flowers beneath his feet,
Nor smelt the perfume, warm and sweet,
That prayed for pity everywhere.
He came to a field that was harried
By iron, and to heaven laid bare:
He shook the seed that he carried
O'er that brown and bladeless place.
He shook it, as God shakes hail
Over a doomèd land,
When lightnings interlace
The sky and the earth, and his wand
Of love is a thunder-flail.

Thus did that Sower sow;
His seed was human blood,
And tears of women and men.
And I, who near him stood,
Said: When the crop comes, then
There will be sobbing and sighing,
Weeping and wailing and crying,
Flame, and ashes, and woe.

II.

It was an autumn day
When next I went that way.
And what, think you, did I see,—
What was it that I heard,—
What music was in the air?
The song of a sweet-voiced bird?
Nay — but the songs of many,
Thrilled through with praise and prayer.
Of all those voices not any
Were sad of memory:
But a sea of sunlight flowed,
And a golden harvest glowed!

And I said: Thou only art wise—
God of the earth and skies!
And I thank thee, again and again,
For the Sower whose name is Pain.

## XXVII.

## "WHEN THE LAST DOUBT IS DOUBTED."

WHEN the last doubt is doubted,
  The last black shadow flown;
When the last foe is routed;
  When the night is over and gone:
Then, Love, oh then! there will be rest and peace:
Sweet peace and rest that never thou hast known.

When the hope that in thee moveth
  Is born and brought to sight;
When past is the pain that proveth
  The worth of thy new delight:
Oh then, Love! then there will be joy and peace:
Deep peace and joy, bright morning after night.

INTERLUDE.

AS melting snow leaves bare the mountain-side
  In spaces that grow wider and more wide,
So melted from the sky the cloudy veil
That hid the face of sunrise. Land and ledge
And waste of glittering waters sent a glare
Back to the smiting sun. The trembling air
Lay, sea on sea, along the horizon's edge;
And on that upper ocean, clear as glass,
The tall ships followed with deep-mirrored sail
Like clouds wind-moved that follow and that pass;
And on that upper ocean, far and fair,
Floated low islands all unseen before.
Green grew the ocean shaken through with light,
And blue the heavens faint-flecked with plumy white.

Like pennants on the wind, from o'er the rocks
The birds whirled seaward in shrill-piping flocks:
And through the dawn, as through the shadowy night,
The sound of waves that break upon the shore!

# PART IV.

I.

## SONG.

LOVE, Love, my love,
  The best things are the truest!
When the earth lies shadowy dark below
  Oh then the heavens are bluest!
Deep the blue of the sky,
  And sharp the gleam of the stars,
And oh, more bright against the night
  The Aurora's crimson bars!

## II.

## THE MIRROR.

THAT I should love thee seemeth meet and wise,
So beautiful thou art that he were mad
Who in thy countenance no pleasure had;
Who felt not the still music of thine eyes
Fall on his forehead, as the evening skies
The music of the stars feel and are glad.
But o'er my mind one doubt still cast a shade
Till in my thoughts this answer did arise:
That thou shouldst love me is not wise or meet,
For like thee, Love, I am not beautiful.
And yet I think that haply in my face
Thou findest a true beauty—this poor, dull,
Disfigured mirror dimly may repeat
A little part of thy most heavenly grace.

## III.

## LIKENESS IN UNLIKENESS.

WE are alike, and yet—oh strange and sweet!—
Each in the other difference discerns:
So the torn strands the maiden's finger turns
Opposing ways, when they again do meet
Clasp each in each, as flame clasps into heat;
So when my hand on my cool bosom burns,
Each sense is lost in the other. So two urns
Do, side by side, the self-same lines repeat,
But various color gives a lovelier grace,
And each by contrast still more fine has grown.
Thus, Love, it was, I did forget thy face
As more and more to me thy soul was known;
Vague in my mind it grew till, in its place,
Another came I knew not from my own.

## IV.

## SONG.

Not from the whole wide world I chose thee—
  Sweetheart, light of the land and the sea!
The wide, wide world could not inclose thee,
  For thou art the whole wide world to me.

## V.

## ALL IN ONE.

ONCE when a maiden maidenly went by,
Or when I found some wonder in the grass,
Or when a purple sunset slow did pass,
Or a great star rushed silent through the sky;
Once when I heard a singing ecstasy,
Or saw the moon's face in the river's glass—
Then I remembered that for me, alas!
This beauty must for ever and ever die.
But now I may thus sorrow never more;
From fleeting beauty thou hast torn the pall,
For of all beauty, Love, thou art the core;
And though the empty shadow fading fall,—
Though lesser birds lift up their wings and soar,—
In having thee alone, Love, I have all.

## VI.

## "I COUNT MY TIME BY TIMES THAT I MEET THEE."

I COUNT my time by times that I meet thee;
These are my yesterdays, my morrows, noons
And nights; these my old moons and my new moons.
Slow fly the hours, or fast the hours do flee,
If thou art far from or art near to me:
If thou art far, the birds' tunes are no tunes;
If thou art near, the wintry days are Junes,—
Darkness is light, and sorrow cannot be.
Thou art my dream come true, and thou my dream,
The air I breathe, the world wherein I dwell;
My journey's end thou art, and thou the way;
Thou art what I would be, yet only seem;
Thou art my heaven and thou art my hell;
Thou art my ever-living judgment day.

## VII.

## SONG.

YEARS have flown since I knew thee first,
And I know thee as water is known of thirst:
Yet I knew thee of old at the first sweet sight,
And thou art strange to me, Love, to-night.

## VIII.

## THE SEASONS.

O STRANGE Spring days, when from the shivering
ground
Love riseth, wakening from his dreamful swound
And, frightened, in the stream his face hath found!

O Summer days, when Love hath grown apace,
And feareth not to look upon Love's face,
And lightnings burn where earth and sky embrace!

O Autumn, when the winds are dank and dread,
How brave above the dying and the dead
The conqueror, Love, uplifts his banner red!

O Winter, when the earth lies white and chill!
Now only hath strong Love his perfect will
Whom heat, nor cold, nor death can bind nor kill.

## IX.

## "SUMMER'S RAIN AND WINTER'S SNOW."

SUMMER'S rain and winter's snow
With the seasons come and go;
Shine and shower;
Tender bud and perfect flower;
Silver blossom, golden fruit;
Song and lute,
With their inward sound of pain:
Winter's snow and summer's rain;
Frost and fire;
Joy beyond the heart's desire,—
And our June comes round again.

## X.

## THE VIOLIN.

BEFORE the listening world behold him stand,
The warm air trembles with his passionate play;
Their cheers shower round him like the ocean spray
Round one who waits upon the stormy strand.
Their smiles, sighs, tears all are at his command:
And now they hear the trump of judgment bray,
And now one silver note to heaven doth stray
And fluttering fall upon the golden sand.
But like the murmur of the distant sea
Their loud applause, and far off, faint and weak
Sounds his own music to him, wild and free—
Far from the soul of music that doth speak
In wordless wail and joyful ecstasy
From that good viol pressed against his cheek.

## XI.

## "MY SONGS ARE ALL OF THEE."

My songs are all of thee, what though I sing
  Of morning when the stars are yet in sight,
  Of evening, or the melancholy night,
  Of birds that o'er the reddening waters wing;
Of song, of fire, of winds, or mists that cling
  To mountain-tops, of winter all in white,
  Of rivers that toward ocean take their flight,
  Of summer when the rose is blossoming.
I think no thought that is not thine, no breath
  Of life I breathe beyond thy sanctity;
  Thou art the voice that silence uttereth,
And of all sound thou art the sense. From thee
  The music of my song, and what it saith
  Is but the beat of thy heart, throbbed through me.

## XII.

## AFTER MANY DAYS.

Dear heart, I would that after many days,
  When we are gone, true lovers in a book
  Might find these faithful songs of ours. "O look!"
  I hear him murmur while he straightway lays
His finger on the page, and she doth raise
  Her eyes to his. Then, like the winter brook
  From whose young limbs a sudden summer shook
  The fetters, love flows on in sunny ways.
I would that when we are no more, dear heart,
  The world might hold thy unforgotten name
  Inviolate in these still living rhymes.
I would have poets say, "Let not the art
  Wherewith they loved be lost! To us the blame
  Should love grow less in these our modern times."

## XIII.

## WEAL AND WOE.

O HIGHEST, strongest, sweetest woman-soul!
Thou holdest in the compass of thy grace
All the strange fate and passion of thy race;
Of the old, primal curse thou knowest the whole:
Thine eyes, too wise, are heavy with the dole,
The doubt, the dread of all this human maze;
Thou in the virgin morning of thy days
Hast felt the bitter waters o'er thee roll.
Yet thou knowest, too, the terrible delight,
The still content, and solemn ecstasy;
Whatever sharp, sweet bliss thy kind may know.
Thy spirit is deep for pleasure as for woe—
Deep as the rich, dark-caverned, awful sea
That the keen-winded, glimmering dawn makes white.

## XIV.

## "OH, LOVE IS NOT A SUMMER MOOD."

I.

Oh, Love is not a summer mood,
Nor flying phantom of the brain,
Nor youthful fever of the blood,
Nor dream, nor fate, nor circumstance.
Love is not born of blinded chance,
Nor bred in simple ignorance.

II.

Love is the flower of maidenhood;
Love is the fruit of mortal pain;
And she hath winter in her blood.
True love is steadfast as the skies,
And once alight she never flies;
And love is strong, and love is wise.

## XV.

## "LOVE IS NOT BOND TO ANY MAN."

I.

Love is not bond to any man,
  Nor slave of woman, howso fair.
Love knows no architect nor plan:
    She is a lawless wanderer,
    She hath no master over her,
    And loveth not her worshipper.

II.

But though she knoweth law nor plan—
  Though she is free as light and air—
Love was a slave since time began.
    Lo, now, behold a wondrous thing:
    Though from stone walls she taketh wing,
    Love may be led by a silken string.

## XVI.

## "HE KNOWS NOT THE PATH OF DUTY."

He knows not the path of duty
  Who says that the way is sweet;
But he who is blind to the beauty,
  And finds but thorns for his feet.

He alone is the perfect giver
  Who swears that his gift is nought;
And he is the sure receiver
  Who gains what he never sought.

Heaven from the hopeless doubter
  The strong believer makes:
Against the darkness outer
  The light God's likeness takes.

Like the pale, cold moon above her
  With its heart of the heart of fire,
My Love is the one true lover,
  And hers is the soul of desire.

# AFTER-SONG.

## AFTER-SONG.

THROUGH love to light! Oh wonderful the way
That leads from darkness to the perfect day!
From darkness and from sorrow of the night
To morning that comes singing o'er the sea.
Through love to light! Through light, O God, to thee,
Who art the love of love, the eternal light of light!

www.ingramcontent.com/pod-product-compliance
Lightning Source LLC
LaVergne TN
LVHW010242110826
845151LV00004B/1364

* 9 7 8 1 4 2 5 5 2 3 2 4 4 *